Praise for
Seasons of Sorrow

If ever there was a book Tim Challies needed to write, it's this one. And it's a book I needed to read. For when afflictions multiply, turning chronic and debilitating, the weary heart longs for some fresh balm to soothe the pain. I found that healing salve in *Seasons of Sorrow*. With heart-shredding honesty, my friend Tim offers robust, Spirit-blessed comfort—the kind that shores up your soul and makes you stronger to endure. Within these pages, you will do more than enter Tim's story of enormous loss; you will come out on the other side having gained a softer heart and a renewed courage to persevere through your own dark seasons of affliction.

> **JONI EARECKSON TADA**, founder of the
> Joni and Friends International Disability Center

Seasons of Sorrow is a beautiful book. Reading it is like holding a precious gift, like standing on holy ground. The death of a child is a stark, shocking, and sad reminder that we do live in a broken, fallen, and groaning world. But it is in these very moments—when the unexpected and unwanted things enter our door, with the darkness of pain, grief, and questions unanswered—that the gorgeous truths of the gospel shine the brightest. *Seasons of Sorrow* will bring you to tears, but through those tears you will see your Lord and the majesty of his grace in ways you may have never seen before.

> **PAUL DAVID TRIPP**, pastor, speaker,
> author of *New Morning Mercies* and *Suffering:
> Gospel Hope When Life Doesn't Make Sense*

I always love reading anything Tim Challies writes, but *Seasons of Sorrow* cut straight to my soul. I read it within a few weeks of the unexpected deaths of two close friends and while my wife struggles bravely with stage 4 cancer. Tim's heartfelt pain and Christ-centered perspective spoke to both my heart and my head. He writes with honesty, authenticity, and depth. There is no pretense here, no airbrushing death or minimizing it. Yet it is a hopeful book that embraces the blood-bought promises of God that one day he will reverse the curse and swallow up death forever. I highly recommend *Seasons of Sorrow* to anyone who has experienced heart-crushing loss.

> **RANDY ALCORN**, author of
> *Heaven* and *If God Is Good*

Tim Challies has taken us into his confidence by writing with such self-searching honesty. It is a painful pleasure to be invited into these sacred moments of grief and to be helped by the reminder that God is too kind ever to be cruel and too wise ever to make a mistake.

> **ALISTAIR BEGG**, senior pastor, Parkside Church,
> and host of the *Truth for Life* radio program

In *Seasons of Sorrow*, Tim Challies bares the heart of an earthly father, utterly crushed by the sudden death of his beloved son, Nick. But as Tim writes out his faithful agony, he also takes us to the faithful joy that can only come from the resurrected Christ. Believers need this book, and only Tim Challies could have written it. I am so thankful that Nick was a student at Boyce College, and his influence as a young Christian was remarkable. Through this book, his remarkable life, joined to his father's God-honoring grief, stands as a testimony to the redeeming love of our heavenly Father.

> **ALBERT AND MARY MOHLER**

In the winter of his sorrow, Tim Challies writes that he wants to be found to be a good steward of what God entrusted him, not in the life, but in the death of his son. And surely this tender book is evidence of that stewardship. As he expresses his agonies and questions and aims, he does the work of discipling all who walk the path of losing someone they love to the anguish of death. In the pages of this book, grieving people will find companionship, insight, and genuine encouragement for the journey.

NANCY GUTHRIE, author of *Hearing Jesus Speak into Your Sorrow* and cohost of Respite Retreats for grieving parents

This book is brilliant, not because of Tim Challies's eloquence, but because of his tears! Many of us have benefited immensely from the author's blogs. However, in this book, Tim takes us even deeper as he wrestles with the brutal ugliness of death during one whole year of personal sorrow after the loss of his son Nick. The buoyancy of faith that shines from every page often left me teary-eyed, thanking God for his grace to his people during their darkest times. What priceless grace!

CONRAD MBEWE, pastor of Kabwata Baptist Church and founding chancellor of the African Christian University

If you have lost a loved one to death, as everyone has, or if you have buried a child, as many have, Tim Challies is your friend. Your brother. Your lifeline. In this poignant collection of reflections, you will grieve with Tim and Aileen and their precious family. Their faith and courage will bless you with an infusion of the same. And their hopeful perspective will help carry you until that day when, as Tim writes, every sorrow will be "comforted in the place where all tears are dried."

ROBERT AND NANCY DEMOSS WOLGEMUTH, bestselling authors

seasons *of* sorrow

—

the pain of loss and the comfort of God

TIM CHALLIES

ZONDERVAN
REFLECTIVE

ZONDERVAN REFLECTIVE

Seasons of Sorrow
Copyright © 2022 by Tim Challies

Requests for information should be addressed to:
Zondervan, *3900 Sparks Dr. SE, Grand Rapids, Michigan 49546*

Zondervan titles may be purchased in bulk for educational, business, fundraising, or sales promotional use. For information, please email SpecialMarkets@Zondervan.com.

ISBN 978-0-310-13675-0 (audio)

Library of Congress Cataloging-in-Publication Data

Names: Challies, Tim, 1976- author.
Title: Seasons of sorrow : the pain of loss and the comfort of God / Tim Challies.
Description: Grand Rapids : Zondervan, 2022.
Identifiers: LCCN 2022009829 (print) | LCCN 2022009830 (ebook) | ISBN
    9780310136736 (hardcover) | ISBN 9780310136743 (ebook)
Subjects: LCSH: Children—Death—Religious aspects—Christianity. | Loss (Psychology)—
    Religious aspects—Christianity. | Grief—Religious aspects—Christianity. |
    Bereavement—Religious aspects—Christianity. | Challies, Nicholas Paul, 2000-2020.
Classification: LCC BV4907 .C47 2022 (print) | LCC BV4907 (ebook) | DDC 248.8/66
    —dc23/eng/20220325
LC record available at https://lccn.loc.gov/2022009829
LC ebook record available at https://lccn.loc.gov/2022009830

Published in association with the literary agency of Wolgemuth & Associates.

Cover design: Brand Navigation
Cover photo: © Marina Zakharova; Arteria Lab / Shutterstock
Interior design: Kait Lamphere

Printed in the United States of America

23 24 25 26 27 28 29 30 31 32 /LSC/ 15 14 13 12 11 10 9 8 7 6 5 4 3 2

This book is dedicated to
Nicholas Paul Challies
March 5, 2000–November 3, 2020

A portion of the author's royalties from this book
are being donated
to the Nick Challies Memorial Scholarship
at Boyce College
and The Southern Baptist Theological Seminary.

Parts of this work appeared,
in various forms and to various degrees,
at Challies.com.

contents

fall

winter

spring

summer

November 4, 2020

In all the years I've been writing, I have never had to type words more difficult, more devastating than these: Yesterday the Lord called my son to himself—my dear son, my sweet son, my kind son, my godly son, my only son.

Nick was playing a game with his sister and fiancée and many other students at his college in Louisville, Kentucky, when he suddenly collapsed, never regaining consciousness. Students, paramedics, and doctors battled valiantly but could not save him. He's with the Lord he loved, the Lord he longed to serve. We have no answers to the *what* or *why* questions.

Yesterday Aileen and I cried and cried until we could cry no more, until there were no tears left to cry. Then, later in the evening, we looked each other in the eye and said, "We can do this." We don't want to do this, but we *can* do this—this sorrow, this grief, this devastation—because we know we don't have to do it in our own strength. We can do it like Christians, like a son and daughter of the Father who knows what it is to lose a son.

We traveled through the night to get to Louisville so we could be together as a family. And we ask that you remember us in your prayers as we mourn our loss together. We know there will be grueling days and sleepless nights ahead. But for now, even though our minds are bewildered and our hearts are broken, our hope is fixed and our faith is holding. Our son is home.

—*Blog entry at Challies.com*

prologue

"we did everything we could"

Things happened that evening that I can barely bring myself to remember, much less to describe in any detail. Much of it has blessedly disappeared from my memory and must have been erased by some kind of a self-protection mechanism within. What remains is isolated fragments, tiny vignettes. I remember receiving the phone call every parent dreads—the one in which a doctor says, "We did everything we could." I remember the anguished cry of a mother who has been told that her son has died and the piercing wail of a sister who has learned that her brother will not come home. I remember the traumatized face of another sister who had watched her brother fall to the ground and die before her eyes. I remember words of disbelief escaping my own mouth: "My boy. My boy. My poor, poor boy." These are sacred moments, haunting memories, that are best left where they are, buried deep within, to rise only amid infrequent flashbacks and disturbing dreams of the night.

But even as the skies went dark that evening, there began to flare up distant glimmers of light, for amid the grief I also remember love. Friends hastened to our side, summoned by the only words we could speak: "We need you." As we wept together, they began to comfort and console us, to speak the highest truths to our deepest sorrows. A mighty chorus of prayer began to be lifted to the heavens on our behalf. As we sat in numb disbelief, a determination arose within us to endure this sorrow well, to face it with faith. The pieces fell into place so we could depart immediately from our home in Canada to be with our daughter in Louisville. Through it all, God was so gentle, so kind, so present—present through his Spirit and present through his people.

In the skies somewhere over Ohio, in the dim light of a darkened aircraft, I began to write. I have often said that I don't know what I think or what I believe until I write about it. Writing is how I reflect, how I meditate, how I chart life's every journey. And so when the sorrow was still new in my heart, when the tears were still fresh in my eyes, when I barely knew up from down and here from there, I began to write. I *had* to write because I had to know what to think and what to believe, what to feel and what to do. I had to know whether to rage or to worship, whether to run or to bow, whether to give up or to go on. I had to know how to comfort my wife, how to console my daughters, how to shore up my own faith. I put fingers to keyboard and pen to paper to find out.

I wrote for my family. I wrote for my friends. I wrote for myself. I wrote my praise and my lament, my questions and my doubts, my grief and my joy. I wrote through depths of sadness and heights of joy, through terrible fears and agonizing pain. I wrote through seasons of sorrow.

———

Some of what I wrote in the year that followed this evening was shared with the public on my personal website, Challies.com. Most of it was not. In this book, I trace my journey through four seasons, beginning in the fall and advancing through winter, spring, and summer. It ends exactly one year after it began, on the first anniversary of the death of my beloved son, Nicholas Paul Challies.

fall

unnatural

I awoke this morning with a tear in my eye. I awoke thinking—or was it dreaming?—of a day long ago when Nick was just a little boy. He was only three years old at the time, and he had just become aware of the existence of death. But his capacity to wonder and to fear was far greater than his capacity to understand.

Aileen was at a Bible study that day and had taken baby Abby with her, so Nick and I had time to ourselves. We settled onto the couch to watch a children's movie together, and inevitably, as it drew to its close, one of the central characters died. I found myself watching Nick as much as the movie while this unfolded. I could see his body begin to quiver as the sorrowful soundtrack swelled. I could see tears begin to form in his eyes as he watched the loved ones gather around their fallen friend. I could see his face begin to crumple and fall.

He turned to me and, with tears spilling down his cheeks, sobbed. "Daddy, why did he have to die? When is he going to come alive again?" I gently pulled Nick onto my lap and, holding him tight in my arms, reminded him of heaven. I told him that heaven is a place where God lives, where there is no more fighting, no more dying, and no more sadness. I told him that it is a place where boys and their daddies can be together forever. He tried to understand, but how is a three-year-old mind supposed to grasp a concept as unnatural as death, as wonderful as heaven?

And so we sat on the couch and we wept together. Nick put his head in my lap and cried about something he could not understand, something he was not created to understand. I stroked his hair and wept for this world—a world that was created perfect but has long since been defiled by sin and death. I wept that a mere child needed to concern himself with matters so sad, so scary, so tragic.

I asked Nick if I could pray with him. Wiping the tears from his cheeks, he said yes and closed his eyes. So I asked God if he would help Nick understand that death is not something to be feared if we love him. I asked God that Nick would trust Jesus to forgive his sins. And, of course, I asked God to comfort Nick so that his young heart would not be troubled but be at peace.

And later that day, I sat at my desk and wrote these words: "I wish I could explain to my son about the death of death accomplished through the death of Jesus Christ. I wish I could make him understand that if he places his trust in Jesus, he has nothing to fear in life or in death. I hope, I trust, I pray that such an understanding will come in due time, so that when someday Nick's eyes close in death, he and I will be reunited in that place where death will be no more, where there will be no more mourning, pain, or sorrow and where God will have already wiped away the tears that filled his little eyes."

I would never have imagined that it would not be me waiting for Nick in heaven, but Nick waiting in heaven for me. But I am certain he will be, for just a few years after this, he decided he would live according to the Christian faith and toward the purpose of making known the goodness and mercy of God. He put his faith in Jesus Christ. He came to believe that Jesus could give meaning and purpose to his life and a good and glorious future after his death. Of course, he didn't know how short that life would be and how close that future was. He couldn't have known. But that didn't keep him from preparing himself.

It became Nick's confidence, Nick's sure conviction, that when his body died, his soul would carry on, that when his body would be buried in the ground, his soul would go to be with God. And though for a time body and soul would be torn apart, a day would come when they would be reunited. The hope his Christian faith offered him is not of a future in which humanity becomes disembodied souls or angelic beings or a part of the cosmos, but something so much better, something so much more fitting for our humanity. The Christian faith offers the promise of a future in which this earth will be renewed and restored, in which all pain and sorrow will be comforted, in which all evil and sin will be removed. And it is in this glorious context that our bodies and souls will be reunited so we can live here in this beautiful world, but with no fear of sickness, no fear of sorrow, no need for three-year-old boys to weep about death, no possibility of twenty-year-old men falling to the ground to die.

It was not my wish that Nick would live so short a life. It is not my wish that I now have to go on without him. The loss is painful beyond any I've ever known and is causing me to cry out from the deepest parts of my being. But I cannot and will not mourn as one who has no hope, who has no confidence, who has no assurance, for I have great hope, great confidence, great assurance, because Nick was ready. Even though he was young, he was ready to die. He had settled the state of his soul. He had prepared for the day of his death.

And so I know in my heart of hearts that I have said good-bye *for now*, that I have said farewell *for a while*, that Nick has not been sent *away* but merely sent on *ahead* to that place where death is no more; where mourning, pain, and sorrow are gone; where God has already wiped away every tear; and where my son is now waiting safely and patiently for his father to join him.

CHAPTER 2

obituary

he ran his short race well

Nicholas Paul Challies was born at Hamilton's McMaster Hospital on March 5, 2000. He was a trailblazer of sorts—the first child to Tim and Aileen; the first grandchild to Mike, Marg, John, and Barbara; the first nephew to Andrew, Maryanne, Emily, Susanna, and Grace.

When Nick was just a few months old, his family settled in Oakville, a suburb of Toronto, where they were joined by Abby in 2002 and Michaela in 2006. He was a quiet and thoughtful boy who valued a small group of friends and a big library of books. He had the precociousness that often comes with being a firstborn, and the sense of responsibility that often comes with being an older brother. He was loyal to his family, kind to his sisters, and honoring to his parents.

Central to Nick's life was his Christian faith. When he was still young, he decided it would be disingenuous to simply imitate his parents in their religious convictions, so he began an independent investigation to determine for himself if the gospel was worth believing. He eventually became convinced that Jesus Christ is the Savior of the world and that he ought to be a follower of Jesus. He professed faith and was baptized and received as a member of Grace Fellowship Church, where he joyfully worshiped and served.

When it came time for him to consider a vocation, he found his heart set on pastoral ministry. His search for a seminary led him to Louisville, Kentucky, and the twin institutions of Boyce College and The Southern Baptist Theological Seminary. In 2018, he enrolled in an accelerated program that would allow him to complete a bachelor's degree at Boyce and, concurrently, a master's degree at Southern, in only five years. He pressed hard, determined to finish early, and was on track to finish in only four. He was a diligent student who developed a particular fondness for New Testament and Greek language studies. He also hit his stride relationally, developing many meaningful friendships, becoming an assistant resident advisor and international student advisor, and taking on the role of mentor to several of the younger students.

Soon after arriving in Louisville, Nick set his heart on Anna Kathryn Conley, who goes by "Ryn." They began dating in 2019 and Nick slipped an engagement ring onto her finger in the opening days of their junior year. Their wedding day was to be May 8, 2021.

On November 3, 2020, while participating in a sports activity with his hall, Nick collapsed very suddenly and unexpectedly. Despite the best efforts of friends, first responders, and emergency room doctors, he could not be revived.

All who had the privilege of knowing Nick grieve his passing and remember him with fondness. All who share his faith commend him for running his short race well and anticipate the day they will see him again. His parents, sisters, and fiancée say, through tears, "The Lord gave, and the Lord has taken away; blessed be the name of the Lord."

CHAPTER 3

in the deepest darkness

My uncle once asked me if I'd like to join him for an afternoon of sailing. He had recently finished restoring a boat, one
styled after the ships of the ancient Vikings, and he was eager
to see how it would perform. We launched the *Perle*, his little
Norwegian faering, into one of Eastern Ontario's innumerable
lakes, clambered aboard, and set out. The sails caught the wind,
and we pushed steadily westward. But as the day continued
and the shadows lengthened, the wind fell off and our progress
halted. A dead calm settled in as night fell, and clouds rolled in
to blanket the moon and the stars. We were now stranded far
across the lake with no wind to drive us, no landmarks to guide
us. We lowered the sails, lodged the oars, pointed the bow in the
direction of home, and began to row. What else could we do?

A darkness overcame me the night Nick died. Up to that
point, my life had largely been bright and easy. But the world
around me began to grow hazy when I heard he had collapsed,
and it grew dimmer still when I was told he had been rushed
to hospital. The doctor's pronouncement of his death was like

11

a heavy darkness creeping in and settling around me, dulling my senses, trapping me in shadow. Though my eyes may have remained clear, my mind has not. My heart has not. Everything is muffled and distorted. Things that should be easy are difficult. My memory is full of holes. I've lost the ability to make decisions. I'm lost, I'm confused, I'm discombobulated, I'm so very weary.

I can remember people talking about how in times of great emotional trauma they were overcome by a kind of dullness, a sense of shock. I'm troubled when I remember them saying it lasted for weeks or even months. I once slipped on some seaside rocks and knew from the unmistakable *crunch* that I had broken my arm. What fascinated me was that for a few minutes, I felt nothing. It was only when the adrenaline wore off, when the shock cleared away, that the dull ache progressed to a sharp pain. The body seems to protect itself that way. Maybe the mind and heart do as well. Maybe this darkness is a blessing, a veil of protection.

In this dim fog, I still don't fully believe that Nick is gone. I don't trust myself to believe it. Even though I am the one who wrote his obituary, I find myself reading it again and again to ensure that it's all true. I've gone so far as to pinch myself, to ask Aileen to assure me I am awake. What if I nodded off and this is all just an awful dream? What if I've fallen sick and this is some feverish nightmare? What if I mistakenly popped the wrong pill and am now hallucinating? Aren't those scenarios more likely than a young man just falling down dead? I tap Nick's name into my computer and find a news story: "Heartbroken Boyce

College Students Mourn the Abrupt Death of Nick Challies."[1] So it is true. But somehow it still wouldn't shock me if my phone rang and I saw his name on the display and heard his voice. I'm hovering in this place between belief and disbelief, between certainty and doubt. I don't know what to think. I don't know what to do. I don't know what to feel.

I don't even know what to feel about my faith, about my God. I should pray, shouldn't I? But I don't find anything to say. I should open my Bible, right? But I can't focus on the words. My eyes flit about, skimming over chapters and verses, but never pausing long enough to absorb a thing. I feel so much and so little. The pain is searing and dull. I'm writhing in agony and lying still, crying and laughing, rejoicing and lamenting. What am I supposed to do? How can I orient myself when everything is so dim, so dull, so dark?

My mind goes back to that evening on the lake so many years ago. The darkness was deep and the wind was calm. We could get home only by rowing. The strange thing about rowing is that oars need to be pulled, not pushed, so progress can come only when the rower turns his back to his destination. I dutifully turned my back to home and put all my strength into pulling the oars. While I rowed, my uncle went to the stern to take the helm. I watched as his experienced hand guided us through waters that were strange to me but familiar to him. He led us past the dangerous shoals, around the protruding rocks, through the narrow channels. My back was still turned when we reached the safe, deep, open waters. His hand was still on the tiller when the bow finally touched the shore and we were home.

I know I am heading into a future that is utterly unknown, utterly foreign, utterly opaque. I am heading into a future I cannot see and will not see until future has become present and present has become past. A wise man once said that the true victory of faith is to trust God in the dark and through the dark.[2] I trusted God as he led me through daylight; I will trust him now as he leads me through the thickest darkness. I may not be able to see the way I go, but I don't need to, because my eye is fixed on the one who is guiding me there. He has given me every reason to trust him. He has given me every reason to have confidence that he will hold my course steady until the keel of this weather-beaten little boat has finally nudged against the shore of glory and I am home.[3]

good night, till then

"Mr. Challies, we want you to know that we have received Nick into our care. Rest assured that he is in the very best of hands."

The message from the funeral director comes as a relief, for it means that Nick's long, last, lonely journey is complete. Even if he can't come home, his body has at least arrived back in his own country, back in his own town. It is not as we hoped. It is not as we imagined. It is not as we wished. But it is as God willed.

"Have you chosen the clothes you'd like him to wear?"

The question seems equal parts significant and ridiculous. How can it possibly matter what he wears in a closed casket? Yet how could we not clothe him in something smart, something dignified, something befitting his humanity?

We choose a handsome gray sweater, well-worn jeans, casual shoes. Rummaging through the basement, we find a bag to hold it all. We fold each piece of clothing carefully, a neat pile, one item upon another.

"Once we have prepared him, would you like to see him?"

We haven't seen him in three months, not since the start of the semester. Should we see him one last time?

We ponder the idea for a few moments but decide, no, we don't want to see him there. We don't want to see him like that. Not as our final memory. We have better memories. Happier ones. We even have photos of him in that very outfit, and in those photos his eyes are open, his cheeks are bright. His fiancée is on his arm and he is joyful, satisfied, content. If all we can have is memories, we prefer to hold on to those ones.

The clothes sit by the door for a day or two, waiting for someone to pick them up. And now, at last, the driver is on his way. Still, I can't shake the feeling that something is missing, that I've left something undone, incomplete.

I go to my office and open the cupboard where I keep my writing paper. I began writing Nick letters in the first days of his freshman year—bits of advice, assurances of love, words of encouragement. I wanted to be sure he'd never have reason to doubt my joy, my pride, my affection. He kept each one. I found them stored together in a little pouch in his dorm room desk. Perhaps, then, it would be fitting to write one more.

In the back of the cupboard I find a notecard embossed with my name. Fitting. I pause for a moment to consider: Is there any good reason to write a letter that no one will ever read? Am I writing for him or for me? Does it even really matter?

I think back to words I had written a year earlier—words of a father reassuring his son, rejoicing in his son. Now I write them a second time:

I love you as much as any father can love a son;
I'm as proud of you as any father can be proud of a son;
I miss you as much as any father can miss a son.

Something is still missing. But what? Words come to mind, lyrics from an old hymn, forgotten to most but precious to me. It's a hymn written from the perspective of a Christian who is spanning that briefest of moments between life and death. I sing it quietly to myself.

I journey forth rejoicing
From this dark vale of tears;
To heav'nly joy and freedom,
From earthly bonds and fears;
Where Christ, our Lord, shall gather
All his redeemed again,
His kingdom to inherit—
Good night, till then!
Good night, good night, good night, till then!

The hymn continues with a second stanza. As this beloved saint draws his final breath, he offers tender assurance to his loved ones:

Why thus so sadly weeping,
Beloved ones of my heart?
The Lord is good and gracious,
Tho' now he bids us part.

Then come words that suit both the one departing and the one remaining. They are just right. Perfect. I take up my pen and write words I imagine Nick is saying to me even as I say them to him:

> Oft have we met in gladness,
> And we shall meet again,
> All sorrows left behind us—
> Good night, till then!
> Good night, good night, good night, till then![1]

"Love forever, Dad," I add. Then I fold the paper and place it tenderly in his pocket. I gently run my hand over the sweater, feeling it one last time—the closest I can come to feeling him one last time. "Good night, my boy," I whisper. "Good night, till then."

from grave to glory

My life has known no moment harder than this. My heart has known no sorrow deeper than this. Nothing could be more final, nothing more sobering, nothing more shattering than watching my son's casket be lowered, inch by inch, foot by foot, until at last it comes to rest at the bottom of a grave. His grave. His place of final rest. I stand with my arms around my two girls, tears coursing down my face, turmoil ravaging my heart. My poor boy. My precious boy. I hear the pastor say the words, "Dust to dust." A piece of me is being buried. A piece of my heart. A piece of my soul. A piece of my very self.

Yet even while all this is true, amid the death, amid the grief, amid the sobs, I can sense something arising, something swelling. Deep in the darkness, almost imperceptibly, something is stirring to life. It is a hope. It is a longing. It is a determination. Though my eyes are fixed on the dirt, my heart is fixed on Christ.

This cemetery is on the edge of town, and just beyond it is what remains of the local farmland. Though most of it has long since fallen into the hands of developers, a few determined farmers have held firm and continue to work their fields. Just a few weeks ago, in the last days of summer, as the weather turned from warm to cool, their tractors began to crisscross these fields, steadily sowing fresh seed.

It might have seemed strange for farmers to sow their seed so late in the year, the earth already beginning to harden and snow soon to bury their fields beneath great drifts. But the farmers made no mistake, for they were sowing their winter wheat. Such wheat is planted in the final days of summer and lies buried in the fields through the cold, dark months. At Thanksgiving, Christmas, New Year's, and Easter, it may appear to have been wasted effort. But the farmers know better, for as winter draws to a close, as the snows melt and the ground warms, that wheat will burst to life and begin to grow. What is sown in the season of cold and darkness will be a rich harvest in the season of warmth and brightness.

Jesus once said, "Unless a grain of wheat falls into the earth and dies, it remains alone; but if it dies, it bears much fruit."[1] For there to be fruitfulness, there must first be death. When skeptics confronted the early Christian leader Paul about the resurrection, he echoed his Savior: "What you sow does not come to life unless it dies."[2] For a seed or a grain to grow, it must first be buried in the ground, where it looks for all the world like it has died. But it is through that process of "death" that it truly comes to life. For a seed to become a plant, for it to bear fruit, for it to really live, it must first die. And so too with human beings.

The hope rising in my heart as I watch my son being sown into the earth is the hope of resurrection. This is not a fingers-crossed, wish-upon-a-star kind of hope, but a sure and steady conviction that what is sown perishable will be raised imperishable, that what is sown in dishonor will be raised in glory, that what is sown in weakness will be raised in power.[3]

I believe and profess, with my son and with the church of all ages, that Jesus Christ was crucified, died, and was buried. But I also believe that on the third day he rose from the grave, ascended into heaven, and is now seated at the right hand of God the Father Almighty, soon to judge and forever to reign.[4] Christ's resurrection is the prototype and guarantee of every Christian's, for Christ's body, too, was rendered lifeless; his body, too, was swallowed up by the earth; his body, too, began to break down and suffer the effects of death. But he was like a seed buried in the ground, for new life soon overtook his death. His soul returned to his body, breath returned to his lungs, a beat returned to his heart. He was raised in power, raised in glory, raised imperishable. He is the firstfruits of a coming harvest.

Those farmers who sowed their fields in the last days of summer are not concerned for their crops through the winter. They know that seedtime and harvest, cold and heat, summer and winter, day and night—these cycles do not cease.[5] They wait patiently and confidently, knowing that soon enough the seasons will change, the sun will warm, the ground will thaw, and their winter wheat will grow into a mighty summer harvest. On that day, there will not be one single stalk in the entire field that did not first have to go into the ground and "die" through the long dormancy of winter's cold.

I can learn from their confidence, for as death is the way to life for a kernel of wheat, death is the way to life for the soul of a human being. I can be certain that right now, though Nick's body is being sown into the ground, his soul has entered the hallowed halls of heaven where there are none but those who came to glory through the grave.[6] There is life after death, but that life must come through death.

asleep in jesus

When Nick was tiny, I often had to stroke his head to get him to sleep. My hand would begin on the crown where his soft hair was only just beginning to grow, then move slowly down his forehead and gently across his eyes to draw them closed. When I reached his little chin, my hand would rise back to the top of his head and repeat the motion again and again. His eyes would slowly grow heavier, his body would gradually relax, and he would finally fall asleep in my arms.

The Bible uses different metaphors to describe the reality of death, but none is as familiar and comforting as the image of sleep. When Jesus heard the news that dear Lazarus had died, he said, "Our friend has fallen asleep." Stephen, when facing the wrath of the mob, cried out with a loud voice and then "fell asleep." Paul was concerned that the struggling church in Corinth would think, wrongly, that dead believers had perished rather than simply falling asleep.[1] Thus, to use the Bible's language, Nick "fell asleep" a short time ago.

Asleep. It's a comforting thought, for sleep is a friend to humanity, not an enemy. When I'm weary, I crave sleep. When I'm homesick, I long to return to the comfort of my own bed. When I'm ill, I long to be tucked beneath warm blankets. Sleep promises relief from so much of what distresses and afflicts us. Night and bed beckon at the close of each long day, extending the warm invitation to lay my weary head on my pillow and simply sleep.

I cling to the reality that Nick is asleep. This pilgrimage is so difficult, this life so tiresome, our enemy so unrelenting. It's a grueling task to wage the long war against the world, the flesh, and the devil, and I find it comforting to know that he is at rest from it all. His burdens have been relieved, his eyes have been dried, his tired feet have been soothed. By falling asleep at such a young age he has avoided so much pain of loss, so many pangs of sorrow, so many aches of aging. He has been freed from the sins that tempted him and the self-loathing that so often dogged him. He has escaped this place of weariness and gone to the place of rest. The poet Ben Jonson wrote these words upon the death of his own firstborn son:

> Will man lament the state he should envy?
> To have so soon 'scap'd world's and flesh's rage,
> And if no other misery, yet age?

Thus, "rest," he could whisper to his boy:

> Rest in soft peace, and, ask'd, say, "Here doth lie
> Ben Jonson his best piece of poetry."[2]

Like the poet's Benjamin, my Nick is at rest. He is asleep. Yet I'm relieved to know it is merely his body that sleeps, not his soul. Though his body lies in the grave, his soul has gone to be with Christ—the Christ who once assured a dying man, "Today you will be with me in paradise."[3] Not some day, but today— this very day! There was not a moment lost between Nick falling asleep on earth and awakening in heaven. No sooner had his eyes closed here than they opened there, to be face-to-face with the Savior of his soul. The apostle Paul insisted that "to live is Christ, and to die is gain."[4] There is gain to be had in death, and it's the gain that comes when we are released from all that is evil and awakened to all that is good. I would not summon Nick back to this world if I could, for that would be to rob him of the greatest of all gains and to force him to experience so much loss.

My mind drifts back to the days when Nick was four or five years old. He went through a phase in which he suddenly dreaded falling asleep, fighting to keep his eyes open, fighting to keep his senses clear, fighting to remain awake. Night loomed like an enemy that would swallow him up, not like a friend that would welcome him. I knew his fears were unfounded, that he would sleep only as long as the short night and then awaken, refreshed in the light of morning. But he was just a little thing with a childish mind and a vivid imagination. My father's heart went out to him in sympathy. I would lie beside him in his little bed, my body pressed up against his. I would sing to him, pray with him, and gently rub his back until his fears were assuaged, until his heart was at peace, until he would finally drift off and be at rest. Then I'd quietly rise, carefully tuck the blankets around him one more time, kiss his forehead ever so gently, and leave him to sleep soundly, to sleep safely, through the night.

I know that Nick is once again merely asleep, briefly asleep, for sleep is a temporary, not permanent state. We sleep for a while, not forever. We rest through the watches of the night, but we awaken with the dawn. At this moment, Nick's body is resting in the dust from which humanity was formed. It may lie there for months or years or centuries, but I have every confidence that a day is coming when the sound of a trumpet will pierce the sky, when the voice of an archangel will shake the earth, and in that very moment, Nick will awaken.[5] He will rise from his rest. His sleeping body will be resurrected to be reunited with his living soul, and he will be alive forever through the endless ages to come. He will wake! He will live! *Maranatha* has been the cry of God's people through the millennia.[6] "*Maranatha*! Come, Lord Jesus! Come quickly!" Come, and wake him from his sleep!

god is good all the time

I've heard of an old man, a stalwart of the Christian faith, who slipped from earth to heaven with the words of a child's song upon his lips: "I have decided to follow Jesus, no turning back." I've heard the account of a renowned theologian who summarized his entire life's work in a melody he learned upon his mother's knee: "Jesus loves me, this I know, for the Bible tells me so."[1] Sometimes the simplest words are the most important. Though we hike beyond theological foothills to explore the towering mountains of God's thoughts and deeds, we never forget the beauty, never stop needing the blessing, of the simplest truths.

I once attended a church where it was the custom of the pastor to pause in his liturgies or sermons to say, "God is good," to which the congregation would reply, "All the time." Then he would say, "All the time," and the congregation would answer, "God is good." It was a recital of the simplest of truths— that goodness is not an occasional attribute of God, not an infrequent disposition, but a constant one. It was meant to remind us that God's goodness does not vary with our circumstances but is fully present and on display in our worst moments as well as our best, in our most lamentable experiences as well as our most joyful. And though the pastor's little phrase may have become trite over time, though I may have grumbled about it in the past, today, right now, nothing is more precious to me, nothing is more important to me, than this: God is good all the time, and all the time God is good.

This is not the only truth that is propping me up. I've heard people in grief speak of God's sovereignty, perhaps repeating a well-known phrase that compares it to a pillow upon which the child of God rests his head, giving perfect peace.[2] Sovereignty speaks to power and the right to reign. It is the attribute of kings or potentates or others in positions of supremacy. Ultimately, it is an attribute of God himself, who rules heaven and earth to such a degree that nothing happens or can happen apart from his will. Nothing is given to us that does not pass first through God's own hand.[3] God's sovereignty is a sweeping doctrine that touches every aspect of life across every moment of creation and every corner of the universe. There is no moment, no spot, no deed, no death, that falls outside of it.

God's sovereignty is offering me comfort in these dark days. It assures me that there was no earthly power, no demonic power, no fate or force above or below, that had its way with my boy, that interrupted or superseded God's plan for him. There was no moment in which God turned his back or got distracted with other affairs or nodded off to sleep. There was no medical deformity or genetic abnormality that had been overlooked by God. God's sovereignty assures me that it was ultimately no one's will but God's that Nick lived just twenty short years, that he died with so much left undone, that he has departed and we have been left here without him. When Job was told of the death of his children, he did not say, "The LORD gave, and *the devil* has taken away," but "The LORD gave, and *the* LORD has taken away." And with that certainty he blessed the name of that Lord.[4]

But while God's sovereignty offers comfort, it offers comfort only if I know something more, something of his character. After all, God might be sovereign and capricious. He might be sovereign and selfish. He might be sovereign and arbitrary. He might be sovereign and evil. So for this reason I ask, "What else is true of God?"

If I am laying my head on any pillow in these days, it is the pillow of God's goodness. I keep saying it: "God is good all the time." I may be saying it with sorrow and bewilderment and something less than full faith. I may be saying it as a question: "God is good all the time, right?" But I am saying it. I don't necessarily understand how God is good in this, or why taking my son is consistent with his goodness, but I know it must be. If Nick's death was not a lapse in God's sovereignty, it was also not a lapse in his goodness. If there was no moment in which God stopped being sovereign, there is no moment in which he stopped being good— good toward me, good toward my family, good toward Nick, good according to his perfect wisdom. God can't not be good!

God's goodness means that everything God is and everything God does is worthy of approval, for he himself is the very standard of goodness. Those things that are good are those things that God deems good, that God deems fitting, that God deems appropriate. For something to be good is for it to meet the approval of God, and for something to meet the approval of God is for it to be good.[5] If that's the case, then who am I to declare evil what God has declared good? Who am I to condemn what God has approved? It falls to me to align my own understanding of goodness with God's, to rely on God's understanding of good to inform my own. Ultimately it's to agree that if God did it, it must be good, and if it is good, it must be worthy of approval. To say, "Thy will be done," is to say, "Thy goodness be shown." It's to seek out evidence of God's goodness even in the hardest of his providences. It's to worship him, even with a broken heart.

Many years ago, I staked my life, my soul, my eternity, on the claims of the Christian faith. I declared that this God was not only *the* God, but *my* God. I acknowledged his sovereignty and his goodness, his right to rule in the ways he deems good, in the ways he deems best. I have never doubted that God's sovereignty and goodness were displayed in giving me my boy. I am fighting right now to never doubt that God's sovereignty and goodness have been displayed in taking away my boy. He was a gift I received with such joy, such gratitude, such praise. He was a gift I am releasing with such pain, such sadness, such sorrow. But as much as I can, I am releasing him with confidence that somehow his death is an expression of the good sovereignty of a good God. This is the God who does all that he pleases, and for whom all that he pleases is good. As I blessed him in the giving, I will bless him in the taking, for he is good all the time and all the time he is good.

only ever an onlooker

There is no place I love more than the mountains, no place where I have a greater awareness of God's power or a more elevated sense of God's majesty. Even the night sky glittering with a host of stars cannot compare to a towering mountain for sheer grandeur. If the heavens declare the glory of God and the skies above proclaim his handiwork, so too, surely, do the great mountain ranges, with their sheer faces, soaring peaks, and quiet valleys. It is difficult to think great thoughts of myself or to take pride in my own accomplishments when I stand silently, humbly, before such undeniable evidence of the creative power of God.

With the grief and chaos of memorials and funerals behind us, we have escaped to the Rocky Mountains of Western Canada. We feel the need to be away from our home, away from our memories, away for a time of reflection, a time of prayer, a time of rest. It is early in the morning and Aileen and the girls are still asleep, but I've awoken in the wee hours to go explor-ing. Dawn is breaking as I drive along a lonely road, climbing, always climbing, ascending one of Alberta's many mountains. Hearing a familiar sound, I pull to the side of the road and exit my vehicle. An alpine stream is flowing nearby, cascading down from the snowmelt above. It splashes steadily downward, dancing over solid rocks, past fallen trees, and cutting beneath this narrow track.

Leaving my car behind, I follow the stream as it descends, noticing how it sometimes disappears into the gullies it has carved into the face of the mountain. At times its sound grows dim as it fades from view. But then, with a rush, it flows out from where it has been hidden, once again both visible and audible. How many hundreds of years, how many thousands, does it take for water to erode rock? How much force must it have? How much strength?

I have gone far enough. I'm not dressed for a serious hike, so I pause my feet and use my eyes to trace the course of the stream rushing downward. Far beneath me, I can see the point where it empties onto the valley floor, becoming a river that flows softly into a quiet, calm lake. I take note of the contrast between the water on the mountain and the water in the valley—water that is rushing, frenzied, disordered, and water that is peaceful, placid, still. It's the same water. But it must endure a harsh journey down before it can flow peacefully again at the foot of the mountain.

My soul feels like the cascading stream, not the peaceful river in the valley, right now. I am deeply troubled, painfully afflicted, sorrowfully uncertain. Questions keep repeating in my mind. *Why me? Why us? Why has God chosen this for us? Why has God chosen us for this?*

In the hidden recesses of my heart, I realize I have begun to blame myself. I can't shake the feeling that Nick's death stems from something I did or something I failed to do—some sin on my part, some lack of conformity to the law of God, or some rebellion against the will of God. I've read deeply from the old devotional writers, the Puritans and their successors, and am struck by how often they write about "afflictions." They often attribute life's trials to God's fatherly chastisement, to divine correction designed to steer us from a destructive course. After all, doesn't the Lord discipline the one he loves, and chastise every son whom he receives?[1] *Could it be that Nick's death is God's discipline toward me? Could it be that Nick was some kind of idol in my life, and to loose my grip on him, God took him away? Could this all be my fault?* I'm haunted by these thoughts and questions.

And then the mountains give me my answer. They remind me of my own smallness, my own insignificance. I am not enthroned at the center of the world and was not enthroned at the center of Nick's existence. He was his own man, his own individual. He was God's son more than my son, God's creation more than my procreation. Nick's death was primarily a transaction between God and Nick, not between God and me. There is a sense in which I was only ever an onlooker in his life and only ever an onlooker in his death. In reality, not even Nick was enthroned at the center of his own existence. He existed according to the plan and purpose of God in order to advance the plan and purpose of God. God was at the center of Nick's life, which means God's purposes are at the center of Nick's death. From all we know of the character of God and his posture toward his creation, and especially toward his children, those purposes must be good, for God can do no evil, wish no evil, want no evil.

That's not to say I wouldn't like to know God's purposes or that I don't find myself tempted to speculate. It could be that God took Nick out of his sheer delight in him. After all, if I delighted in the son whom I received from the hand of God, how much more delight must there be in the heart of the God who made him? Or it could be that God took Nick to spare him from something else. Weren't there many times when I as a father inflicted minor pain on my son—perhaps through fatherly discipline or through the jabs and pokes of vaccinations—to later spare him more significant suffering? Or could it be that God took him so that many would hear of his Christian faith and be inspired or that his family could suffer their grief well and testify to God's grace even in the midst of searing loss? Doesn't the world often scorn professions of faith in Christ and look on skeptically when Christians suffer, expecting they will now abandon the faith they profess?

Perhaps it was one of these or all of these and many more, for I am convinced God is usually achieving not one thing or two or three, but a thousand or two thousand or ten thousand. A little mind like mine cannot hope to put all the pieces together, to unweave the entire tapestry or make sense of the whole. But I can have complete confidence that it is all according to the good plan of a good God, a God whose heart is always love, whose purpose is always love, whose acts are always love, whose very nature is love.

It falls to me, then, not to take blame for what happened, nor to attempt to determine God's reasons for it, but simply to accept this as his will—his divine will, his secret will, his good will. There is much that God aims to teach me through it, I am sure. But I need to be careful to distinguish the purposes from the results, why God did it from how God will use it. I'm certain he will use this to better equip me to live for the good of others and the glory of God. He will use it to work within me greater love, joy, peace, patience, kindness, goodness, faithfulness, gentleness, and self-control.[2] He will use it to further conform me to the image of his Son. But I have no need to insert myself between God and Nick as if I am the one who caused his death, as if God took him because of me. Rather, I must allow his death to make me godlier, to make me holier, and then to love and serve all the more.

Deep within me, the cascade has fallen to the valley floor and emptied into the still waters. My soul has been quieted, and an old hymn rises within, a hymn of confidence, a hymn of peace:

> Be still, my soul; the Lord is on your side;
> bear patiently the cross of grief or pain;
> leave to your God to order and provide,
> in ev'ry change he faithful will remain.
> Be still, my soul; your best, your heav'nly Friend
> through thorny ways leads to a joyful end.[3]

I turn around, retracing my path, an old song in my heart, a new spring in my step.

my manifesto

By faith I will accept Nick's death as God's will, and by faith accept that God's will is always good. By faith I will be at peace with Providence, and by faith at peace with its every decree. By faith I will praise God in the taking as I did in the giving, and by faith receive from his hand this sorrow as I have so many joys. I will grieve but not grumble, mourn but not murmur, weep but not whine.

Though I will be scarred by Nick's death, I will not be defined by it. Though it will always be part of my story, it will never become my identity. I will be forever thankful that God gave me a son and never resentful that he called him home. My joy in having loved Nick will be greater than my grief in having lost him. I will not waver in my faith, nor abandon my hope, nor revoke my love. I will not charge God with wrong.

I will receive this trial as a responsibility to steward, not a punishment to endure. I will look for God's smile in it rather than his frown, listen for his words of blessing rather than his voice of rebuke. This sorrow will not make me angry or bitter, nor cause me to act out in rebellion or indignation. Rather, it will make me kinder and gentler, more patient and loving, more compassionate and sympathetic. It will loose my heart from the things of earth and fix it on the things of heaven. The loss of my son will make me more like God's Son, my sorrow like the Man of Sorrows.

I will continue to love God and trust him, continue to pursue God and enjoy him, continue to worship God and boast of his many mercies. I will look with longing to the day of Christ's return and with expectation to the day of resurrection. I will remain steadfast and immovable, always abounding in the work of the Lord.[1] I will forget what lies behind and strain forward to what lies ahead, always pressing on toward the prize of the upward call of God in Christ Jesus.[2] I will lay aside every weight and sin that clings so closely and run with endurance the race that is set before me, looking always to Jesus, the founder and perfecter of my faith.[3] I will remain faithful until I have fought the good fight and finished the race and kept the faith.[4] I will die as I have lived—a follower of Jesus Christ. Then, by grace, I will go to be with Jesus, and go to be with Nick.

This is my manifesto.

singing in the dark

"How are you doing?" I've been asked that question countless times lately. I never really know how to answer it. While at this exact moment I may be doing okay, it's possible that fifteen minutes earlier, I was so overwhelmed with sorrow I could barely stand. It's possible that fifteen minutes later, I'll be reveling in the joy of knowing my son is safely home in heaven. I can go from joy to sorrow and back again in moments. How am I doing? Most of the time I don't even know. And if I don't know, what hope do I have of expressing how I feel to anyone else?

I've found help in an ancient proverb—a proverb that addresses my inability and perhaps my frustration with that inability: "The heart knows its own bitterness, and no stranger shares its joy."[1] I take this to mean that some sorrow is so bitter, so painful, so deep, that it simply cannot be expressed to anyone else. Sometimes there are, quite literally, no words. I can press into the proverb a little more to consider why this is. It must be because the one experiencing the sorrow cannot articulate their grief, even to themselves. It's the *heart* that knows its own bitterness, not the mind, not the tongue. This grief is lodged deep in the soul, inexpressible by mind or mouth.

Though I am a writer by trade, though words are my currency, I still lack the ability to express the deep sorrow of losing a child. How can I express the anguish of watching my firstborn be lowered into the cold ground, the agony of choosing the words that will be etched onto the gravestone of my only son, the torment of knowing that behind a still-closed bedroom door is all that evidence of a life lived and lost? How can I express what it means that his sweet fiancée will never be my daughter-in-law, that I will never be able to hold my son's sons, that I will grow old without the one who promised to always take care of me? Truly, the sorrow is not only beyond description but also beyond my own comprehension.

Yet I'm confident there is one who understands what I cannot. God reveals himself as the good Father who searches and knows the deepest recesses of my heart. His Son is the very Man of Sorrows who is intimately acquainted with grief and who can sympathize with me in my every weakness. And his Spirit, I am assured, intercedes with groanings too deep to utter, too deep for words.[2]

I've found special comfort in these, the Spirit's groanings, for I am often unable to do little more than groan, sigh, and sob. My prayers are often devoid of words, yet still full of meaning, full of significance. Sometimes the best I can say is, "God! God! You know." The words are simple, plain, and monosyllabic, but they emerge from the depths of my soul. It's a blessing to have this assurance that the Spirit is committed to helping me in my weakness. It's a comfort to know that he is in the business of understanding and interpreting what I find inexpressible. It's consoling to know that God cares, that God hears, that God knows.

The heart knows its own sorrow, its own bitterness, says the proverb. But sorrow has not been my only experience. Far from it! One of the realities of grieving as a Christian is the coexistence of heights of joy alongside depths of sorrow. They run in parallel, like two streams flowing from a common mountain peak and traveling through the same valley, yet never quite touching, never quite emptying into the sea to become one. The proverb acknowledges this, for it reminds me that what is true of sorrows can also be true of joys. Just as I cannot adequately describe the sadness, I also cannot adequately describe the happiness. How could I express my delight in knowing that Nick is in the presence of God, my pride that he finished his race well, my pleasure in hearing so many people describe his kind deeds and godly character? Both the laughter and the tears are beyond my ability to describe, not just to others, but even to myself.

While the streams of joy and sorrow run in parallel, they are not identical. The stream of joy is more like a gentle brook, while the stream of sorrow is like a raging river. It is sorrow, not joy, that threatens to overwhelm me, pull me in, and drag me under. I've never had to remind myself to temper my joy with sorrow, but I have often had to remind myself to search for light amid the darkness. And it's in this dichotomy that Charles Spurgeon has proven helpful, for he once preached a sermon on this proverb and pointed out that God has promised his people that joys will always attend their sorrows, for "the deeper the waters, the higher our ark mounts towards heaven. The darker the night, the more we prize our lamp. We have learned to sing in the dark with the thorn at our breast."[3]

And so I press on, singing in the dark, with the lamp of the Lord illuminating the way. Despite the pain, despite the sorrow, despite the loss, my life goes on. It must go on. I know I won't ever get over it, but I do need to get on with it, for I haven't received an exemption clause that frees me from what God has called me to.[4] I am still a father, still a husband, still a pastor, still a friend, still a neighbor. While Nick may have been taken, I have been left. While his race may be complete, mine continues. This loss has scarred me, but it does not define me. Life must still be lived. Songs must still be sung.

i fear god and
i'm afraid of god

The fear of the Lord is the beginning of wisdom.[1] And fear is the beginning not only of wisdom but also of the Christian life. The Bible makes it clear that to love God, to honor God, to obey God, we must first fear God. But *fear* is a word with many dimensions, many definitions. In what ways are we to fear God?

Theologians have long distinguished between the fear of a slave and the fear of a son. A slave will naturally and rightly fear an evil master who is inclined to lash out in wrath toward him. The slave will grovel and plead, hope and beg, to stave off the whip, to be spared harsh and unjust suffering. The fear of a son could not be more different. An honorable son will also naturally and rightly fear a kind and loving father, but his motivation is not the fear of consequences, but the desire to avoid bringing shame or reproach on the one he loves. If he feels anxiety, it is not from fear of torture or punishment, but from fear of displeasing and dishonoring the father who has so often and so lavishly proven his love.[2]

I have feared God in this way since I was young. From the time I was a child, my parents made the proverbs part of my spiritual diet, so that I have always known the importance of having a healthy fear of God. I have taught my own children, "Blessed is the man who fears the LORD, who greatly delights in his commandments!"[3] To honor God we must fear God—to have a deep and abiding sense of God's power, God's majesty, God's holiness, God's sheer otherness. We live best when we live with a healthy fear of God.

So I do fear God. But these days I also find myself just plain afraid of God. I fear him in that sense of rightly assessing his power, his abilities, his sovereignty. But I'm also afraid of the ways he may exercise them. After all, just a short time ago, God exercised his sovereignty in taking my son to himself. My life of ease and privilege was interrupted by a loss so great I would never have allowed myself to even imagine it. In one moment, God delivered a blow that staggered me, that very nearly crushed me.

It was God's right to take Nick. I know that. I affirm that. The God with the ability to give is the God with the right to take. Willing as I was to receive Nick as a gift from God's hand, I cannot and will not begrudge the same God for taking him back. Like Job, I blessed the name of the Lord in the giving and will bless it still in the taking.

But it is God's ability and willingness to take that leaves me fearful. For if Nick's life was so very fragile that it could end in a moment without obvious cause or explanation, why not the lives of others who are precious to me? If God has called me to suffer this blow, why not another? If God took my beloved son with such speed, with such ease, with such finality, what else might he take? Who else might he take? And how could I bear up under such a loss?

I am not particularly prone to anxiety, to fretting, to irrational fears, but in these days I find myself living with a sense that something bad is about to happen. Or that it could happen, at least. There's a cloud on the horizon, a soundtrack whose notes have become foreboding, alarming footsteps approaching in the dark. I don't want to let my girls out of my sight. I don't want Aileen to venture anywhere on her own. I don't want any of them to put themselves at even the slightest risk. I'm jumpy. I'm scared. I'm looking over my shoulder. I am quite certain that some of my grief is for losses I've only imagined, losses that haven't even happened and probably never will.

It's silly to think that I could somehow prevent these losses by acting in a controlling way. It's irrational. Nick was the most cautious of our children and was taking no risks when his life came to an end. There was no connection between what he was doing and why or how God took him. And we know that since God had determined Nick's time was up, there was no doctor who could heal him, no procedure that could restart his heart, no medicine that could bring him back. It is true of all of us that nothing can end our lives before the moment God has ordained, and then nothing can save them.

But still I fear. And when I'm honest with myself, I admit

that it is God I'm afraid of. I'm afraid of what else he might call me to do. I'm afraid of what other ways he might exercise his sovereignty. I'm afraid of what else he may will for me to endure. It's not that I begrudge or distrust him. At least, I don't think so. I'm in awe of his ability and his willingness to work his will. But I'm also intimidated by it, afraid of what it might take from me.

Perhaps the reality is that I fear God in a new way and that some kind of innocence has been shattered. Before Nick's death, I understood that God had power, but now I *know* that he has power. Before, I understood that God would exercise his power in giving what I love, but now I understand that God will also exercise his power in taking what I love. Before, life was easy because God's sovereignty always seemed inclined toward the things I wanted anyway, but now life is hard because I see that God's sovereignty may also be inclined toward the things I dread, the things I would never wish for.

I choose to submit myself to that sovereignty, to continue to pray, "Thy will be done." But even as I pray, I cringe just a little. I pray the words with little faith and with some hesitation. I pray them as much because I know they are the right words to pray as because I really want God to act on them. Even as I recite the words, at least for now, I feel some measure of dread. For I know that God *will* carry out his will—his good will—no matter what it gives to me or takes from me. It's the taking I fear. And behind the taking, the Taker.

winter

turning to face the sun

Winter has come to Canada. The days are now short. The air has become cold. The first snow has dusted the ground. Outdoor activity has given way to indoor lethargy. We have added extra blankets to our beds, replaced cotton sheets with flannel, dug out the warm winter pajamas. Hats, gloves, and scarves are readied by the door. The fire is dancing on the hearth as we settle in to wait out another long, cold winter.

We who live in cold-weather climates could be forgiven for thinking that the sun is cooler in winter than summer, that it must operate on a kind of thermostat that can be lowered for a time, or that for these months it must turn to concentrate its heat on another part of our planet. But the truth is that through all seasons the sun remains fixed at the center of our solar system; through all times it glows at a steady temperature. What changes is not the sun but our position relative to it. It is the earth's tilt and rotation that gives us our seasons, at times causing the sun to beat directly onto its surface and at other times striking it with a glancing blow. The sun's angle is low in a Canadian winter, which makes the days short, the nights long, and the air cool.

As I endure this time of pain and trauma, I am sometimes tempted to feel like God has become distant from me or turned his face away. I sometimes feel as if God's love for me has grown cool. Perhaps he has turned his attention elsewhere or turned down his affections. But then I think of our planet, I think of our sun, and I think of our God.[1] Surely he is not a God who forsakes his people when they need him, his children when they cry out for him. Surely he is not a God who is least present when most needed. He promises that his eye is upon us and his ear is toward us, so when we cry out, he hears and delivers. He promises he is near to the brokenhearted and saves those who are crushed in spirit.[2] Is my spirit not crushed? Is my heart not broken? Am I not crying out? Then surely God is near. Surely God has not turned away. Surely he is not ignoring my cries.

If I feel like God has become distant or cold, is it not more likely that I have changed than God? Surely it cannot be traced back to the Father of lights, with whom there is no variation or shadow due to change, surely not to the one who proclaims so plainly, "I the LORD do not change," to the one who promises that even though heaven and earth will some day pass away, he remains constant, the same yesterday and today and forever.[3]

I am confident that warmth will return to this land, for God has promised that while the earth remains, seedtime and harvest, cold and heat, summer and winter, day and night, shall not cease.[4] The snow will melt, the ground will thaw, the birds will return to the skies, the plants will spring up from the ground. The cool whites and desolate grays will give way to rich greens and bright reds and warm blues. All this will begin to unfold, not when the sun changes, but when the earth once again rotates so that this land faces the full light of the sun, the full strength of its heat.

And I, too, must change my angle, my bearing, my attitude. I realize I have been trusting too much in my feelings and that I must submit them to facts, to truth, to what is eminently more trustworthy. My feelings rotate like the earth; my emotions come and go like the seasons. But the truth is as fixed and constant as the sun. When I focus on what is true, I understand that God is present with me. He has been present since the moment I heard the awful news; he is present with me right now; he will be present with me until that day when he at last wipes away my final tear. He has been particularly present with me through his Spirit and through his people.

As Jesus prepared to leave his disciples all those centuries ago, he promised that in his absence he would send the Holy Spirit. He was true to his promise, and the Spirit now takes up residence within God's people to be our helper, our comforter, our counselor—*my* helper, *my* comforter, *my* counselor.[5] And I know he has been ministering to me, drawing to my mind and illuminating to my heart the truths of the Bible—its sweet blessings, its precious promises, its consoling assurances. Never before has truth been so dear, so important, so soothing. I'm clinging to it, repeating it, preaching it to my own soul. Like a dying man wringing a damp cloth to squeeze its final drops of precious water onto his parched tongue, I'm wringing the Word for every drop of comfort it can provide me. And in his precious, inward way, the Spirit is ministering it all to me.

And as God has been spiritually present through his Holy Spirit, he has been physically present through his people. Brothers and sisters have surrounded me and loved me like I've never been loved before. They've prayed for me and wept with me, bearing my burdens and providing for my needs. The same Jesus who sends the Spirit describes the church as his body, and this body has been his hands, his feet, his arms, his mouth. They've done his work, carried out his mission, ministered his comfort, spoken his words. The voice of God has been the voice of his people, the arms of God the arms of his people. He has been as present as the hands stretched out to provide food, the shoulders offered to cry upon. "I have been young, and now am old," testified David, "yet I have not seen the righteous forsaken or his children begging for bread."[6] Or lacking divine comfort in their deepest afflictions.

For the earth to transition from winter to summer, for it to be transformed from dormancy to fruitfulness, it must turn toward the source of warmth, the source of life. It must turn to face the sun. And I, too, when cool and lifeless, when sorrowful and downcast, must turn to face the God of light and life who is himself a sun and shield, who bestows favor and honor, who withholds no good thing from those who walk uprightly, from those who trust in him.[7] I must face the one who will never leave me, never forsake me. O God, help me to turn and bask in the warmth of the Son![8]

help my unbelief!

It is one of the most poignant episodes from the life of Jesus. A desperate father has come to him for help, for he has a son who, from childhood, has suffered from demonic possession. Not only has some foul demon rendered his son mute, but it has also been convulsing him, casting him to the ground, where he goes rigid, grinds his teeth, and foams at the mouth. He is sometimes thrown into fire and water, where he could be grievously harmed. It is difficult to imagine a more pitiable creature than this young man—or a more anguished figure than his father.[1]

Now this father is before Jesus, and in torment he pleads for help, mercy, and deliverance. "If you can do anything," he cries, "have compassion on us and help us." Jesus picks up on a single little word—*if*. He homes in on it, repeats it, emphasizes it. "*If* you can!" he repeats with a measure of disbelief. "'*If* you can'! All things are possible for one who believes." The father replies with words of faithful honesty, of honest faithfulness: "I believe; help my unbelief!" He has a measure of faith, he knows, but not as much as he would like to have. He trusts God, but his trust is mixed with uncertainty. He has confidence, but he also has doubts. "Help my unbelief," he pleads. "Help me!"

I sympathize with that father. I identify with him. I recognize the existence of his faith, but also its insufficiency. My cry, too, is often, "I believe; help my unbelief!" But where that desperate father was concerned for what was happening to his son's body, I am concerned for what has happened to my son's soul. That father was concerned for what he could see, but this father is concerned for what I cannot see: *Where is my son? What is he experiencing? How can I know that he is okay?*

The same Bible that describes this anecdote from the life of Jesus describes human beings as both bodies and souls. It affirms what we know to be true—that there is more to us than our physical selves. There is a part of us that is immaterial and immortal, a part of us that carries on even when our bodies die. That being the case, I can have confidence that when Nick's body fell to the ground, his soul lived on. But what happened to it? Where is it? Where is he?

I was raised around creeds, confessions, and catechisms—means of concisely summarizing great swaths of biblical teaching—and from my youngest days, I have been taught that, upon death, "souls, which neither die nor sleep, having an immortal subsistence, immediately return to God who gave them."[2] Though Nick's heartbeat was extinguished that day, his soul was not. If the confession is correct, the part of him that carries on was summoned to the presence of God. But then what? Surely not every soul is received with joy, for some people have spent their lives rebelling against God, denying his very existence, perhaps even destroying people made in his image.

The confession continues, saying that "the souls of the righteous being then made perfect in holiness, are received into paradise, where they are with Christ, and behold the face of God in light and glory, waiting for the full redemption of their bodies." The souls of those who are righteous are welcomed into that place we know as "heaven," the paradise where God's people await the day when Jesus Christ will return to earth, when God will create a new heaven and new earth—a new world free from sin, sickness, and death. Was Nick among the "righteous" who had the privilege of being made perfect in holiness and of being received into this paradise? Surely he was, for he had confessed his sins and his sinfulness; he had put his faith in Jesus Christ; he had received the righteousness of Jesus Christ as a gift of grace. He was not a perfect man, but he had been forgiven by one.

And so, according to this confession's summary of the teachings of the Bible, I have every reason to believe that Nick is in heaven, that Nick is holier now than he has ever been and, therefore, happier than he has ever been. I have every reason to believe he is in the presence of God himself. I have every reason to believe he will be waiting there when the time comes for me to join him. I believe it! I believe it! I believe it!

But if I believe it, why do I sometimes not believe it, or, at least, why do I sometimes not believe it as much as I'd like to? Why is my faith sometimes mixed with doubt? Why do I sometimes have to force myself to believe it? Why do I sometimes believe it, not because I am fully convinced of it, but because the alternative is beyond what I can bear? *O God, won't you fill up what's lacking in my confidence? Won't you give me the faith I do not have? I believe! Please help my unbelief.*

CHAPTER 14

what do you do
with grief?

She's so big and so small, so old and so young, so weak and so strong, so brave and so broken. Today she is sprawled all over my lap, her head on my shoulder, her tears cascading to my chest. "I miss him so much," she sobs. The brother who was her dearest friend, her closest confidant. The brother who listened with such patience, who guided with such skill, who loved with such fierce affection. The brother who fell to the ground in her presence, the brother she could do nothing to help, the brother whose life ebbed away before her eyes. It would grieve me to know she had watched a stranger die; it shatters my heart to know she watched her own brother die.

An old song says that love is a many-splendored thing, for love has many hues, many shades, many facets. It has many features to observe, many marvels to behold. There is so much bound up in love that none of us can ever experience it in all its forms and all its glories. The love of a mother is different from the love of a father, the love of a parent from the love of a child. Sister-love is different from brother-love, friend-love from stranger-love. God-love surpasses them all. Many splendors indeed.

I am learning that what is true of love is equally true of grief, for it, too, has many hues, many shades, many facets. The grief of a mother is different from the grief of a father, the grief of a parent from the grief of a sibling. It is experienced differently by each individual and manifests itself in deeply personal ways. Criers cry and brooders brood, emoters emote and thinkers think, extroverts prattle and introverts ponder. Some deny and some accept, some press on and some come to a halt, some cannot stop thinking about it and some cannot bring themselves to think about it at all.

And then while we grieve as individuals, we also grieve as a family, for our loss is common and shared. Nick was torn from *us*, from our little clan, our little household. The griefs even compound in such a way that added to my own sorrow is the sorrow of watching my wife lament her son, of watching my daughters grieve their brother. I would protect my girls from any pain or any sorrow if I could. But there is nothing I can do to protect them from this or to take it from them. There is just so much sadness, and it takes so many forms. It would be hard enough to lead myself through this grief, but I must also lead my wife and my girls. I have never been needed more than I am needed right now. I have never had greater responsibility than at this time of deepest grief. They need me to be available to them, to minister truth to them, to intercede on their behalf.

I recently added the heading "grief" to my prayer lists for Aileen and the girls but find I don't really know what to pray for. I don't really know what the goal is. I don't really know what destination I want to pray them toward. I know what to do with sin: "Put to death therefore what is earthly in you,"[1] says the apostle. So sin is to be put to death. I know what to do with virtue: "Put on then, as God's chosen ones . . . compassionate hearts, kindness, humility, meekness, and patience."[2] So virtue is to be put on. I know what to do with sin and virtue, but what's the right thing to do with grief? Should I pray that they get over their grief? That they work through it? That they rise above it? That they get out from under it? That they put it behind them? Should they embrace their grief or fight it, accept it or reject it? Certainly I can pray that God will comfort them, and I have great confidence that he will. But surely I should be praying for more than that. Surely there are some actions they can take, some verbs I can pray on their behalf.

Perhaps I need to first establish in my mind the nature of grief. Is grief an emotion or a feeling? Is it a thing or a being? Could it be a state or a sin, an origin or a destination? I am coming to understand grief as a response and a process—a response to circumstances and a process that begins with a sore trial or deep loss. And while I am less certain of the destination, I think it must be acceptance, submission, peace, and hope.

And so I find myself praying that Aileen and the girls will accept Nick's death as God's good and perfect will, even if also his inscrutable and difficult will. I am praying that they would bow their knees to the King on his throne, submitting themselves to him and to his right to rule his world in his way. I am praying that the divine peace that surpasses all understanding would calm their hearts and soothe their souls. And I am praying that they would know the sure hope of Jesus Christ and of his precious gospel—the hope that Nick is with Christ and that when they have persevered to the end, they will be with him. I pray that this acceptance and submission will lead to sweet peace and enduring hope.

And then, inspired by the apostle Paul, I find myself praying that they would forget, remember, and press on. I pray that they would forget their grief in the sense that they would refuse to be defined by it or be made useless to the Lord's purposes because of it. I pray that they would remember their grief in the sense that it is now a part of their story and a part that has equipped them for more and better service to God. And I pray that they would press on through their grief, with hearts softened by loss, hands fitted by sorrow, feet running by faith, and arms always straining forward, always pressing on toward the goal for the prize for which God is calling them heavenward.[3]

crying eyes and smiling hearts

We have decided to visit Nick. "Visit Nick"—that's what we've begun to call it when we spend time at his graveside. "Going to the cemetery" focuses on the place, not the person, so it's too impersonal, too abstract. "Paying our respects" is another option, but it sounds too formal to describe going to the place where our son's body lies. So we "visit Nick," which is what we are doing on this Christmas morning.

We slept in for a while, then ate breakfast, then opened gifts. To this point, it has been just like every other Christmas for the past twenty years, save for his absence, and save for a few tears. Now, with those well-worn traditions behind us, we have entered into that lull between our morning routine and our Christmas dinner. And so, rather spontaneously, we don our coats and boots, our hats and mittens, and make the short drive.

Snow has blanketed the town—it began after nightfall on Christmas Eve and ended just as dawn was breaking on

Christmas morning. It covers the ground, of course, but also every roof and every car. It clings to every branch of every tree. It is the most pristinely white Christmas we have ever witnessed. It's a special blessing that's breathtaking in its beauty.

As we arrive at the cemetery we see we are not the only ones to visit a loved one today. Tracks lead from the roadway to this grave and that one, sometimes a single, distinct set of bootprints in the snow, sometimes a jumble of little ones and big ones together. Some have left cards or laid wreaths or lit candles. One has carefully cleared a plot, leaving a rectangular patch of dormant winter grass starkly visible against the surrounding snow.

We blaze a fresh path to the farthest grave, the newest grave, the one that has been there for such a short time it does not yet have a monument or even a marker. The thick blanket of snow makes it impossible to see the disturbance where a hole has been dug and imperfectly refilled. But we know the spot.

We stand for a few moments, arm in arm, tears trickling down our cheeks and splashing to the snow. We try to talk, but what is there to say? I had thought I might pray, to thank God for the precious gift he gave us in so fine a man, so loyal a son, so committed a Christian. But now that it has come to it, I have no words. When I try to open my mouth, little escapes beyond broken sobs. But I'm confident that God hears the prayers I cannot speak. He knows what it is to lose a son.

We have brought a present of sorts—sprigs of the poinsettia that for the past few weeks has brought its wintery cheer to our living room. We kneel beside the grave and place our gifts carefully on the undisturbed snow. They've come from the warmth of our home to the chill of this place. Their little splashes of bright red and green are set against the blinding brilliance of the snow. It isn't much, but it's something. It's from our home. It's from our hearts.

We think of our son and our God-given calling to raise him in the discipline and instruction of the Lord.[1] We think of the tiny baby we carried out of the hospital on a fine March morning so long ago. We think of the boy who awoke to the perilous state of his soul and put his faith in Jesus Christ. We think of the teenager who became so kind, so humble, so committed a Christian. We think of the young man who ran his short race so very well. We think of the son who is now safe at home in heaven. "We did what God called us to do," I whisper. "By grace," Aileen replies.

Our hearts smile, even if our faces do not. We turn and retrace our tracks back to the roadway, back to the van, back to Christmas. We've added a new tradition to our old ones.

CHAPTER 16

the prayer i couldn't pray

Father in heaven, it is the final meeting in our New Year's week of prayer, the evening we dedicate to prayers of thanksgiving. It's a virtual meeting, and on the computer screen before me I see the faces of the people I love, each little square another one of the dear brothers and sisters who together make up Grace Fellowship Church. One by one they pray, offering their words of gratitude, their words of praise for the year that has come and gone. And what a year it was—a year of pandemic and uncertainty, a year of regulations and separations. It was a hard year for everyone in this church, and I'm encouraged as I listen to each one remember your mercies and offer you their thanks.

I want to pray. I genuinely want to give the signal and wait my turn and key my mic, but I find I cannot. I want to express thanksgiving, for I am so very thankful for so very much, but the lump in my throat and the tears in my eyes tell me I lack the ability just now. So please hear this prayer as I tap it on my keyboard.

This was a hard year, Lord, the hardest I've ever known. You know that, for there is nothing that happened in it that was outside of your knowledge. There was not an hour you were absent, not a moment you turned your back. My brightest days and darkest days were alike, each fully known to you. You knew I would begin the year mourning my father. You knew I would end the year mourning my son. You knew that between these times, I, with the rest of the world, would face the confusion and uncertainty of a global pandemic. You knew I would spend weeks and then months in isolation, quarantine, lockdown. You knew that so much of my grieving would be in solitude—few people, few visits, few hugs. You knew. Yet you also knew that through it all, I would experience so much of your mercy, so much of your grace, so much of your love. You knew that time and again, you would prove yourself good and very good. And I'm so grateful.

I visited Nick today, as I do each Sunday. And as I stood by his grave, by that unmarked little patch of disturbed earth where his body lies, I felt gratitude. Even through my tears, even through my sobs, I felt my heart warm with love for you and the gift you gave me. So I want to say thank you. Thank you for giving me my son. Thank you for entrusting him to me. I acknowledge that he was your child before he was my child. You loved him long before I first saw him, first held him, first knew him. Thank you for the honor it was to raise him, to care for him, to love him. Thank you for forgiving him, for saving him. Thank you that though he is not in *my* home, he is in *yours*. Thank you that though he is absent from his body, he is present with the Lord. Thank you for the assurance you've given that you didn't first take him from me, but first took him for yourself. Thank you for the certainty I have that his arrival in your presence was a gain far greater than the loss of his departure from my own.

Thank you that friends have been so faithful to express love and bring comfort through this time. Thank you that mere acquaintances and even strangers have been so kind, so generous, so loving. Thank you that our parents and siblings have been so faithful in caring, so committed in praying. Thank you that Aileen has stood strong in her faith through this harshest of trials, that she has been such an encouragement and inspiration to me. Thank you that Abby and Michaela have deepened their faith through their loss where, had you not held them, they otherwise might have abandoned it altogether. Thank you that you have provided your divine comfort as mediated through human mouths and human hands.

Thank you, Father, that you are sovereign, that this is your world and that nothing within it happens outside of your will. Thank you for the mystery of your providence, through which you guide and direct every life and death toward your great purposes. Thank you that your actions are only ever good, and your timing only ever perfect. Thank you that your heart is always inclined toward your people, always eager to bless, always eager to comfort.

Thank you, Jesus, for being born into this world—God himself taking on human flesh. Thank you that you lived a perfect life, that you died an atoning death, that you rose victorious over the grave. Thank you that you opened the way to God so I could be saved, so Nick could be saved. Thank you that you were and still are the mediator between God and man.

Thank you, Spirit, for being the comforter. Jesus said it's better that he would go so you could come, so thank you that you have taken up residence within and in that way have been so present to guide, to assure, to comfort, to lead away from bitterness and toward holiness, even in the deepest depths of grief.

So, Father, Son, Spirit, thank you that you are God, that you are good. Thank you for all the blessings I've received from your hand. Thank you for the assurance that the greatest blessing is still to come—the blessing of being made perfect and living in your presence forevermore.

And now we are coming to the end of our prayer meeting, the end of our week of prayer, so I close with this: It's my longing to bring glory to your name—my longing to display your power in my weakness, your wisdom in my brokenness. And so I willingly submit myself to your purposes. You are the Creator; I am the created. You are the potter; I am the clay. If I can best bring glory to you through weakness, then I say take my strength; if I can best bring glory to you through poverty, then I say take my riches; if I can best bring glory to you through loss, then I say take it all. I can endure any trial, surmount any suffering, face any sorrow, as long as you do not leave me, as long as you do not forsake me. And you promise you never will. You promise you will work all things for good, and so I ask that you would do that. Work my weakness for good, work my losses for good, work my brokenness for good, for I love you and have been called according to your purpose. Whether this year brings plenty or hunger, whether it brings abundance or need, whether it brings joy or sorrow, life or death, I ask only that you enable me to give thanks in every circumstance, for I know that each one will have been ordained by you. Let me press on toward the prize, and as I do, to bless the Lord at all times, with his praise—your praise—continually in my mouth.

In the name of Jesus Christ, I pray. Amen.

CHAPTER 17

stewarding sorrow

"What are you feeling?" he asks. "How does a father reconcile himself to the loss of a son?" An old family friend has called to check up on me and to assure me that he has been praying for me, for my wife, for my girls. But he is also curious and would like to know what it's like to be in my position. "What's going on in your heart?" I am surprised by the words I hear coming from my mouth. "I feel honored. I feel honored that God has entrusted this to me. I know it comes from his hand, and I want to steward it well."

I have long been taught to interpret life through the lens of stewardship. To be a steward is to be an agent, an overseer, a caretaker. A steward is responsible, not for his own possessions, but for someone else's. He answers not to himself but to a master, a monarch, an owner. Jesus tells a parable about stewardship—about three servants, each of whom is entrusted with a portion of their master's wealth as he departs on a long journey. One is given a single portion of the wealth, another two portions, while the third is given five. Jesus explains the behavior of each of these servants, saying that the two who have been entrusted with much are wise and judicious, doubling what they have been given. But the one entrusted with little is foolish and frugal and in the end has nothing more to show than the bit he began with. At the final accounting, two of these servants are rewarded for their faithfulness—"Well done, good and faithful servant!"— and one is rebuked for his lack of faithfulness—"You wicked and slothful servant!"[1]

I have always known that my children are actually God's children. I don't own Abby, I don't own Michaela, and I never owned Nick. I don't own them any more than I own my money and property, my gifts and talents, my privileges and opportunities. "This is my Father's world," says the hymn writer.[2] My children, no less than the rest, are gifts of God, entrusted to me by his hand. To me he has assigned the responsibility of raising them in the discipline and instruction of the Lord, of stewarding them faithfully as one who will have to give an account.

I often felt honored to have been entrusted with Nick. There were many times when he was a child and teenager, and many more when he was a young adult, that Aileen and I looked at one another and marveled at the gift God had given us. "What did we do to deserve so fine a son?" we would ask each other. "Why would God entrust such a treasure to us, of all people?" He was an abnormally good child, unusually kind and gracious, remarkably dutiful, extraordinarily committed to honoring God. It was an honor to receive him and an honor to raise him. So why should it not be an honor to release him? Why should we not consider it an honor to have been chosen for this difficult calling of letting him go? After all, he was not truly ours to begin with. He was never our possession. He did belong, and he does belong, to God.

As I look anew at Jesus' parable, I'm struck that the servants are never offered a choice in their stewardship. The master never thinks to ask them, "How would you feel about being given one portion or five portions of my wealth?" He never consults with them to ask, "What do you think you're capable of handling?" Rather, he simply assigns to each of them as he sees fit and then expects they will prove themselves worthy of the responsibility he has conferred. The one who receives the five portions must be particularly thrilled, for surely it speaks of his master's confidence in him that he has been entrusted with much rather than little. His master's confidence is a blessing, a reward all its own, and it must spur him on all the more to prove himself faithful, to prove himself worthy of so great an honor.

I've always been convinced that God entrusted us with much in giving us Nick. He was the whole five portions. And today I'm convinced that God has again entrusted us with much in taking him. His death is another five. Maybe even ten. We labored to prove faithful in Nick's life, to raise him in such a way that we would hear our master's commendation. We've been called to a new task now, a new stewardship, and it falls to us to prove faithful in his death. We labored to raise him in a way that brings glory to God; we now labor to release him in a way that brings glory to God. For surely such a weighty calling is a sign of our master's confidence. Surely with such a sobering responsibility comes the promise of great reward, if only we will prove faithful. And what greater reward than to hear, "Well done, good and faithful servants! Enter into the joy of your master"—the joy of our master, the presence of our master, where our child—his child—has gone on ahead.

CHAPTER 18

thy will be done

We prayed as a family before Nick and Abby left for their fall semester, then snapped a photo of the two of them standing together outside our home—our two college students. It was August 1, and they were headed to Louisville, Kentucky, Nick for his junior year and Abby for her freshman. I made the journey with them since these were the early days of a worldwide pandemic, and regulations mandated that foreigners like us quarantine for two weeks upon arrival in the United States. We dutifully stayed isolated together in a borrowed basement apartment until the fourteen days were up, then drove to campus and unloaded a tower of suitcases and boxes. I hugged Nick, told him I loved him, and watched as he walked away arm in arm with the woman who, just weeks later, would accept a ring from his outstretched hand. And that was the last time I ever saw him. It was the last time I ever will see him on this side of heaven.

Abby returned home after the on-campus memorial service and has been with us ever since, waiting out the long winter break between semesters. But now school is opening again, classes are beginning, and we are having to bid her farewell. It's a good thing, we know, but it's also a very hard thing. Abby is booked on the first flight of the day—a short hop to Detroit, where she will be able to connect to Louisville. We got up at 4:00 a.m. to make sure she had time to clear security and customs before her 6:30 a.m. departure. While we were confident her paperwork was in order, we've learned not to take too much for granted when it comes to transiting international borders. Leave two hours at minimum, they advise.

We roll to a stop outside Toronto Airport's terminal 3. Abby has had to pack for two seasons—for a cool southern winter and a warm southern spring. I wrestle two giant suitcases to the ground behind the van and, doing the math, realize they weigh as much as she does. The pandemic continues to rage, and since regulations forbid me from as much as going through the terminal doors, she is going to have to manage them on her own. That doesn't seem fair.

I already know she has her boarding pass and passport with her; I already know she has figured out how to navigate all three airports she'll pass through today; I already know an infatuated young man is eager to pick her up on the far side. I have already prayed with her—Aileen, Michaela, and I had huddled together and prayed for her safety and protection before she headed out the door. So what's left to do but to say a final goodbye?

I do my best to be brave, as I know I won't be doing her any favors if I break down and cry. I take her face in my hands, look her in the eye, and say, "I love you. Be safe. I'll see you soon."

I kiss her on the cheek and then leave her to drag her two full-sized suitcases into the terminal. Climbing back into the van, I have one more prayer: "Nevertheless, not my will, but yours, be done."[1]

My temptation in a moment like this is to be anxious. It's to think of what happened the last time my children headed south, to use my mind to fabricate a vision of a similar future and then to feel all its sorrow, its grief, its trauma—to shed tears over sorrows that may never come. I could cripple myself under the weight of such fantasies. I could crush my spirit. I could commit a slow suicide.[2]

I often sense this temptation building. The first scenes begin to play in my imagination and I have to decide whether I'll let them roll or whether I'll shut them down. I know what Jesus said: "Do not be anxious about tomorrow, for tomorrow will be anxious for itself. Sufficient for the day is its own trouble."[3] I know it's God's responsibility to concern himself with the future, and mine to live well in the present. I know God promises grace sufficient for every trial, but only trials that have actually happened, that exist in the real world, rather than the world of fantasy. I know God's power is made perfect in genuine weakness, not imagined. But still I sense anxiety's tug, still I begin to see those scenes in my mind, to feel them with my emotions, to dread them in my heart.

I have learned that grief is often accompanied by fear and amplified by it. The mother whose son has been struck by a car worries about her other children safely crossing the street; the father whose daughter was killed in a car accident frets every time his remaining children back down the driveway. And I, whose son collapsed and died, cannot fall asleep in the evening until I have received assurance that both my daughters are still alive and cannot be content in the morning until I am sure both have made it through the night. Nick's death has made us face mortality and human fragility in a whole new way. My children may as well be made of glass. I'm just so afraid that if Providence directed I lose one, it may direct that I lose another. If it has determined I face this sorrow, why not many more?

How, then, can I let go of such anxiety? How can I continue to live my life? The only antidote I know is this: deliberately submitting myself to the will of God, for comfort is closely related to submission. As long as I fight the will of God, as long as I battle God's right to rule his world in his way, peace remains distant and furtive. But when I surrender, when I bow the knee, then peace flows like a river and attends my way.[4] For when I do so, I remind myself that the will of God is inseparable from the character of God. I remind myself that the will of God is always good because God is always good. Hence I pray a prayer of faith, not fatalism: "Your will be done. Not as I will, but as you will."

There is comfort in any prayer—comfort in asking God for his care, for his blessing, for his protection. There is comfort in expressing my desires, my preferences, my hopes and plans. But there is more comfort still in wrapping it all in this prayer. I pray it as a profession of faith, an acknowledgment of God's love, of God's goodness, of God's sovereignty. I pray it as a declaration that his knowledge is more expansive than my own, that his will is better than my own, that his wisdom is higher than my own.

So I will pray for the desires of my heart. I will ask God to bless and protect my girl. I'll plead with him to bring her home to me in May. But the steel thread woven through the fabric of such a prayer is not "my will be done" but "thy will be done." Ultimately, if there is to be comfort, it will not be grounded in the hope that nothing bad will happen to me or to the people I love, but in the perfect God whose perfect character is displayed in his perfect will.

CHAPTER 19

to my son on his twenty-first birthday

Happy birthday, my boy! You're twenty-one today! Or you would have been. Do you celebrate birthdays in heaven? Do you even mark days, months, and years? I confess, I have only just begun to realize how little I know about the place you have gone to be. I've got many questions, but few answers. Then again, I could only get credible answers through the Bible, and it seems to be far less concerned with describing lives in heaven than directing lives on earth. It's better that way, I'm sure. I suppose I'll have to wait and get my answers when I arrive.

Speaking of which, I don't really know what it looks like to arrive in heaven. I sure hope, though, that you'll be right there when my time comes. I miss you so much. I miss your voice and smile and laugh. I miss your friendship and conversation and counsel. I miss your wisdom and patience and godliness. I miss being father to a son. Being your dad was truly one of the highest honors I could ever imagine, and outliving you is one of the deepest sorrows. I'm so happy that you're there, of course, but so sad that you're not here. There's a void in my life now. It was a part of me that died that day, a part of myself, the best of myself. You were the best part of me. And I'm sure I won't ever be whole again on this side of eternity.

I'm so proud of you, Nick. I'm proud of the life you lived and the legacy you left. Everyone who knew you has spoken well of you. Friends, neighbors, students, cousins, church members—all spoke of a man who was gentle and kind, godly and good. Your colleagues at the grocery store sent us a book of memories, and so many of them spoke of a man who had been patient and friendly and who had talked to them about Jesus. There was no blame attached to your life, no scandal, no dishonor. We learned secrets about you, but they were all good secrets—about the people you quietly mentored, the prayer meetings only you attended, the people who were overlooked by others but loved by you. You lived with honor and integrity. You died a man of irreproachable character. You ran your short race well.

I probably ought to confess I went through your computer's search history, but only to see if I might dig up some clues about how you died. Maybe you had been searching for symptoms of something. You hadn't, as it turns out, but even there, I found not a single search and not a single site that was anything less than above reproach. It's clear that the man you were in private matched the man you were in public, and that makes my heart swell with pride. I've often thought how much better it is to be the father of a departed joy than of a living sorrow.[1] You brought me such joy in life, and despite all the tears, you've also brought me such joy in your departure.

I do some silly things now, things that would probably make you laugh or maybe just roll your eyes. Like I sometimes brew a cup of coffee for you before I visit the cemetery on a Sunday afternoon. It's absurd, I know, but it reminds me of the hundreds of times I made your coffee before you headed off to work or school. We bonded over coffee—over different flavors, different roasts, different methods of brewing—so I sometimes take you a cup and leave it there. It's dumb, I guess, but who's to judge? And really, one of the hardest parts of my loss is that all my feelings of love remain, but there's no way to express them. For twenty years there was always something I could give you, something I could do for you, some way I could spoil you. But now you are beyond all doing, beyond all need, beyond all expressions of love. It's hard on a dad.

I asked granddad to make a glass case for your Bible, the one I gave you when you decided to go to seminary. I'm going to lay it open to 1 Corinthians 15 (which Dr. Schreiner read so movingly at your memorial service) and keep it near me always. Then whenever I need to, I'll be able to look over and read the great promise that keeps me going: "For as in Adam all die, so also in Christ shall all be made alive."[2] There's such hope there. Such promise. Such joy to look forward to. We will be alive together forever.

You'd be so proud of mom. Even after twenty-two years of marriage, I wouldn't have been able to predict how she would respond to such heartbreak, how she would do with waking up to her worst nightmare, but she's done it with strength, with grace, with godliness. I think that of all of us, she may have endured the hardest loss, for her heart is the most compassionate and was most knit to yours. Who can deny that the two of you shared a special bond? But she is holding fast to truth, preaching it to herself, and ministering it to the rest of us.

You'd be proud of your sisters too. Michaela often cuddles up against me in the evening to cry a little, to express her sorrow but also her hope, acknowledging that this is God's will, so it must be right and good. She looked up to you, she admired you, and she treasures the memory of every one of your kind words and good deeds. Abby has gone back to school and is doing well there. She adored you and regarded you as her closest friend and most trusted confidant. But she, too, has determined that she will trust God in her sorrows just as she has in all her joys. All of us have pledged together to stay true to Christ, true to his gospel, true to the end, so we can all be sure of a great family reunion. What a day that will be!

You'd also be proud of your precious Ryn. Her grief as a fiancée falls into a difficult category. She had decided to live the rest of her life with you, to align her dreams with yours, but had not yet made it official through marriage. So her grief is much like a widow's, but without the level of support and understanding that widows get. But she is strong and godly and enduring her pain. You'd be happy to know that she and mom have become fast friends and talk just about every day. She is bound to our family now, and we hope she will always remain part of it.

I suppose you'd also be glad to know we are all together in Louisville today. We'll spend the day with Ryn, cry a little, laugh a little, and then mom will make the usual Friday evening pizza. We are also going to spend time with some of your friends, who, by the way, are all wearing Blue Jays hats in your honor. You'd be so embarrassed! On Sunday we'll head home, and then I guess life will carry on.

And life has to carry on, doesn't it? What choice do I have but to shoulder this burden, to carry this cross, to press on toward heaven, to press on toward you? God has used your death to help pry my fingers off this world, to make me long for heaven in a whole new way. But he has also used it to give me new directions for life, to make me want to make the most of my time on earth. My longing for heaven is now inseparable from my longing to see you. I can barely wait.

Oh, my Nick, I miss you so much. It has been 203 days since I hugged you goodbye, 124 days since I spoke with you, 122 days since you went to heaven. It all feels so long. But also so short. And I expect the same will be true of the time that elapses between today and the day we're back together. James says life is a vapor, a breath, a puff, a whisper.[3] I'm more mindful of that than ever, that each day is precious, each day is a gift to be used for the good of others and the glory of God. So I prayerfully discern each day's duty and carry it out as best I can. Then, when night comes, I fall asleep thinking, *When I wake up, I'll be one day closer to Nick, and if I don't wake up, I'll finally be with Nick.* And to be honest, I'm okay either way.

I'll see you soon, my sweet boy.

Love forever, Dad.

CHAPTER 20

homesick

My thoughts these days turn often to heaven. In those moments when I hover between asleep and awake, in those moments when I bow my head to pray, in those moments when I lift my voice to sing, my mind turns often to that place and to its people. My father made the journey there not too long ago, and my son trailed close behind him. The two key men in my life—the one in whose footsteps I followed and the one who was following in mine—have both preceded me and both await me. Never have I had such longing to be there, for never have I been able to envision a welcome from those who are so familiar, so beloved, so sorely missed.

The Bible has a lot to say about heaven, and much of it is presented in language that demands analysis and meditation, language that points us to the literal by way of the evocative. Heaven has gates of pearl and streets of gold, we are told. It has walls of jasper and waters of crystal. It is in the shape of a cube, each of its walls adorned with precious jewels. It is bright, but without sun or moon, for God himself is its light.[1] There is a mystery to heaven. It must be so much better than we can imagine, so far beyond our comprehension, that only poetic representations can even come close to doing it justice. And even if these images do not let us perfectly picture it in our minds, they most certainly make us long for it in our hearts.

But there is far less mystery and far more familiarity to the most precious of its descriptions—home. For each of us, the Father has reserved a room in his home, says Jesus, and he himself has gone to prepare it. To leave behind the body is to be at home with the Lord, assures the apostle Paul.[2] And so his longing and ours is to be away from this fragile tent and to be safely delivered to the great home that has been so carefully planned by the mind of God, so carefully constructed by the hand of God. What comfort there is in knowing that when we come to the end of our lives, we do not depart into the ether or disappear into the void, but simply go home.

We all know what it is to be home. Home is the place of safety, the place of security, the place of familiarity. When we have ventured far, we long to return home, for we know we always leave behind a part of our very selves. No matter how joyful a vacation, no matter how wonderful a journey, home always draws us; it always beckons us to return. It is at home that we are always welcome, at home that we love to celebrate, at home that we are most authentically ourselves. Nowhere offers more comfort, nowhere offers more joy, more peace, more love, than home.

And right now I am sick for home. Though at this very moment I'm within the walls of my house, I know this is truly no more than a sojourner's shelter, a spot to rest briefly along the way. For I myself am no more than a pilgrim making a long journey through the wilderness to that glorious promised land, that perfect eternal habitation. Even as I am here, I long to be there. I long to arrive at the banks of the Jordan, to safely cross over, to set my feet upon its banks, to enter the very gates of the Holy City. There is less here to hold me back than ever before, more there to call me onward, to call me homeward, to call me to that place I long to be.

I'm confident that, despite my longing, to be here is more needful than to be there, at least for the moment. God has people for me to love, purposes for me to fulfill, burdens for me to bear. I will continue to prepare myself for the place God has prepared for me, continue to walk the narrow path he has charted for me, knowing that whether smooth or rugged, whether well paved or potholed, this road leads me home. With each step I feel the anticipation growing, with each footfall the homesickness settling deeper within. I long to be home! When the storms of life howl around me, home! When the cares of life threaten to overwhelm me, home! When the losses of life threaten to break me, home! My eyes strain to see it, my ears to hear it, my hands to grasp it. Home, sweet home. Home where my God is. Home where my heart is. Home where my father is. Home where my son is. Simply, wonderfully, eternally home.[3]

flowers in the desert

A number of years ago, Aileen and I realized, rather suddenly, that our children had grown old enough that they could be left on their own for a few days. We were certain the two of us could benefit from some time away, some time by ourselves. We found flights to Arizona, where we could fulfill our dream of exploring some of America's best national parks and finest natural beauty.

And what beauty there was! We hiked the famous Canyon Overlook Trail in the darkness so we could see the sun rise over Zion National Park. Later that day, we watched the same sun set over the red sands of Bryce. We marveled at the Vermilion Cliffs, admired the haunting majesty of the Grand Canyon, and stood in awe of the power of the mighty Colorado. We were struck by the beauty and praised God for his handiwork. Yet as we lay in the darkness of our hotel and planned out the final day of our little vacation, we couldn't shake the feeling that we had somehow missed the best of the beauty.

We decided we would set aside the maps, leave behind the

tourist routes, and give ourselves over to serendipity. Early the next morning, we struck out into the desert, following roads that grew narrower and rougher as they drew us farther off the beaten path. The skies turned dark around us, thunder began to rumble, and a great storm threatened. And it was here and now, far from anyone or anything, that we found the inspiration we had been missing. It was a parched landscape, a vicious sky, a towering cactus, and, set against it all, precious flowers. Under the darkness of clouded skies, set against the stark desert sand, standing before cruel thorns, we found flowers displaying their stunning beauty. Their bright blooms contrasted with the darkened sky, their gentle petals with the sharp thorns, their green leaves with the dry sands. We found flowers in the desert, beauty beneath threatening skies, splendor alongside spikes. We paused, we admired, we delighted. We returned home fulfilled, rejoicing.

God makes many promises, and the best of them are for our worst times. It is when we are struck down and very nearly destroyed that we most crave God's comfort, God's assurance, God's words of peace. Perhaps the most precious of all is this: all things work for good.[1] Those who love God and are loved by him can have confidence that he is working through all of life's circumstances to bring good out of bad, light out of darkness, joy out of sorrow. It's not that God is especially agile, a kind of cosmic PR man adept at manipulating circumstances, but rather that he is the planner, the engineer, the designer, who has ordained the means just as much as the end. He ordains the calm and the storm, the darkness and the dawn, the famine and the feast. This being the case, no event is meaningless, no situation purposeless, no condition ultimately hopeless. God is working out his good will, not despite dark days, difficult trials, and broken hearts, but through them. Such circumstances are the raw material he uses to form and shape his good plans, his perfect purposes.

When Jesus spoke to his disciples on that final evening of his life, he said, "What I am doing you do not understand now, but afterward you will understand."[2] He was about to be betrayed, to be taken prisoner by a mob, to be abandoned and denied by his friends, to be horrifically assaulted and cruelly murdered, to face the pure and holy wrath of God against sin. He was about to endure the most hideous, heartbreaking circumstances of any person at any time in all of history. And to his friends he gave this word of explanation, this word of assurance: Afterward. Afterward you will understand. This would all make sense eventually, but only later. It would all become clear, but only after it was complete. They would need to endure before they could understand. For there to be a glorious Easter Sunday, there must first be a terrible Good Friday and, between them, a bewildering and sorrowful Saturday.

The history of God's work in this world is full of such "afterwards." Joseph had to be for many years a slave before he could be a ruler and declare to his brothers, "God sent me before you to preserve life" and "you meant evil against me, but God meant it for good." Moses's mother had to set him afloat on the river and release him to be raised by a foreign princess before she knew her son would lead the great exodus. Peter had to witness the death of Jesus and endure three days of bewilderment before he could attest that those who had put his Lord to death had done only whatever God's hand and plan had predestined to take place.[3] There was good in all these bads—promises fulfilled, people redeemed, salvations wrought. But the good was bound to the afterward.[4]

"All things for good" is an "afterward" promise, a promise I must take by faith, for it is not always apparent to sight. It's no magical pill to immediately soothe all my pain, no panacea to instantly heal all my wounds, but neither is it meant to be. God's promises settle alongside my pain to strengthen me through it. I lift aching hands in worship, raise a trembling voice in praise, turn tear-filled eyes to the heavens. "All things for good" is God's assurance that if I trust him with the present, he will make good on the future. Stephen was stoned to death, the church was scattered, but the gospel spread with it—God worked it for good! Peter suffered imprisonment, but the church learned the power of prayer—God worked it for good! John was confined to Patmos, but there he received his great vision of the heavenly throne room—God worked it for good![5] There is no circumstance beyond "for the good" because there is no circumstance apart from the definite plan and foreknowledge of God.

And so God has called me to trust him in the dry deserts as in the green pastures, in the tumultuous deeps as in the gentle shallows, in the lowest sorrows as in the highest joys. For God's specialty is not bringing good from good, but good from bad. If I trust him through my tears, I am confident he will give me reason to laugh; if I trust him through my pain, he will teach me to praise; if I trust him through my grief, he will afterward show me all the good that came with it and through it. He will show me the precious flowers in the dry desert, the beautiful blooms against the sharp thorns, the gentle petals beneath the vicious skies. For behind every black cloud is a yellow sun, behind every dark night a bright day, behind every frowning providence a smiling face[6]—the smiling face of the God who works all things for good for those who love him and are called according to his purpose.[7]

spring

not a moment too early

The days are growing longer, the air is getting warmer, and winter is at last giving way to spring. In the fields outside town, a farmer is preparing his land for another season of growth. He has already examined the soil to test its texture and fertility. And now he tills his fields, loosening the soil and turning it over to expose it to sun, rain, and precious nutrients. As soon as he has confidence that we've seen the year's final frost, he will begin to sow his seeds. He grows corn here as well as field crops—carrots, beans, peppers, peas, pumpkins. In just a few weeks, the cold, dark soil will burst to life as the first green sprouts push their way out of the ground.

The farmer knows that his beans will be ready first, for they take just a couple of months to grow and mature. As the weeks pass, he will keep a close watch, examining them for shape, for thickness, for crispness. He will harvest them only when they are just right. The carrots will be ready shortly after and will be pulled from the ground when he is certain they are at their best, their juiciest, their most flavorful. The carrots are followed by the peas, then as summer continues, the peppers and the corn.

Finally, in the first chill of early autumn, he will declare the pumpkins ripe and ready, just in time for Thanksgiving feasts and Halloween frights.

The farmer stops his tractor, climbs down, and digs his hands into the rich earth. He runs the soil through his fingers. He examines it closely. What is he looking for? What is he hoping for? What little prophecy might that soil hold? I know very little about farming and the cycles of sowing and reaping, planting and harvesting. As a city dweller, I trust farmers like this one to plan wisely, to operate judiciously, to supply what I could not possibly provide for myself. I trust him to know when each plant is ready—which ones will be fully grown after seventy days, which will be at their best after eighty, which must wait until one hundred. I trust him to know when each seed is ready to be sown and when each crop is ready to be harvested.

In the stories we are told of Jesus, he often turned to farmers and farming, to plants and soil, to illustrate spiritual realities. "A sower went out to sow," he said. "The kingdom of heaven may be compared to a man who sowed good seed in his field." "Lift up your eyes, and see that the fields are white for harvest."[1] And still today the farm and the farmer pose a question: Shouldn't I trust God to know when each person is ready to be harvested from the soil in which they are grown? Shouldn't I trust God to know when each person is ready to be plucked from the life God himself has given them? For is not a human being of much greater value than a plant, and the wisdom of the Creator much greater than the wisdom of any farmer?

It was my hope and my assumption that Nick would be a

late crop, not an early one, that he would be harvested in the autumn or winter of life, not the first days of summer. I would never have guessed that his time would come before mine, for there is something so unnatural about a father outliving his son. But God must have known better, right? If even the good farmer knows when to harvest each plant, does not our good God know when to summon each of his precious children? Does he not know when each is prepared, when each is mature, when each is perfectly ready to be gathered in? Of course he does.

My challenge is to trust God for my son like I trust the farmer for my food. It would be the height of folly, the height of conceit, the height of presumption, for me to march into the farmer's field and tell him when to till, when to plant, when to sow, when to plow. This is his business, not mine. It is the farmer who has the wisdom to know these things, not me. And in the same way, it would be rash, it would be arrogant, it would be downright blasphemous, for me to demand that God cede to my will, my plan, my desires, my limited grasp of the facts. For matters of life and death fall within the jurisdiction of God, not man. They are the expertise of that Father, not this father.

And so I trust that Nick lived the number of years, days, hours, minutes, and seconds that were perfect for him. His life was not cut short but lived to the final moment of God's good plan. He was kept by God until he was ready to go and ready to be taken, ready to be gathered in. And then God called him home. Like old Enoch, young Nick walked with God and was not, for God took him.[2] In the wisdom of God and according to the will of God, he died not a moment too late, and not a moment too early.

CHAPTER 23

how long is the dash?

Nick's gravestone has finally been installed, and I have come to see it for the very first time. I have been looking forward to this day and dreading this day in equal measure. For months I have had to visit an unmarked grave, a patch of bare earth with no way to identify the name of the precious person who lies beneath it. Surely my son deserves better. Yet now that it comes to it, I also hate seeing his name carved on a slab of stone. There is something unnatural about this. Something so stark. I can't decide if this gravestone is the final honor associated with his life or the final indignity associated with his death.

I read aloud the words I prepared months ago. At that time they were fleeting black characters tapped onto a flickering white screen; now they are permanent white characters etched onto a polished black stone. It was important to me then, and it remains important to me now, that his Christian faith is made as explicit in his death as it was in his life. In a place where so many are buried beneath vapid platitudes and trite iconography,

I want the world to know that this man loved Jesus and has gone to be with him.

NICHOLAS CHALLIES
Mar 5, 2000–Nov 3, 2020

Loyal son to Tim and Aileen,
kind brother to Abigail and Michaela,
devoted fiancé to his beloved Ryn,
faithful follower of Jesus Christ.

He fought the good fight,
He finished the race,
He kept the faith.

My eyes return to those two dates and the dash between them. I wonder: How long is that dash? How long is that single little character we use to separate the date of birth from the date of death? Is it an inch? Is it two? In one sense it doesn't matter. But in another sense it matters a great deal, because encapsulated in that little line is the story of a life lived and then lost, a life begun and then ended, a life celebrated and then mourned. For the old man buried in the plot just beyond this one, the distance between the left and right edge of that dash tell of a full, rich threescore and ten. For the little girl in the next row, it represents mere months. For Nick, it represents twenty years: March 5, 2000–November 3, 2020.

I imagine for a moment that the dashes on every gravestone here could be made proportional to the length of the life lived. Those who died in infancy, whose earthly life was measured in minutes or hours, might have a dash no longer than a fraction of an inch. Those who died in childhood might have half an inch. Nick was given twenty years, so perhaps his could measure the full inch. And so it goes, two inches to the forty-year-old, four inches to the eighty-year-old. Maybe a little bonus could be awarded to the few who reached their hundredth birthday. Had old Methuselah been buried under a headstone here, perhaps his dash would span several feet across an absurdly elongated monument.

And then I wonder, *How long is eternity? How long is forever? What kind of dash might represent the life that has a beginning but no end? How long would be the line that begins on March 5, 2000 and extends for ten thousand times ten thousand years?* That line would extend beyond the edge of this monument, carry beyond the boundaries of this cemetery, and pass the borders of this town. It would reach Canada's beautiful Maritime provinces, stretch across the cold Atlantic, and touch the western shores of Europe. It would carry across the bare steppes of the East, leap the Himalayas, cross the Asian continent, and plunge into the mighty Pacific. After thousands of miles across the deep ocean floor, it would gain land again, cross Canada's prairies, and finally return once more to Oakville. But even then, it would be only getting started, for it would begin another circumnavigation of the planet, then another. It would stretch endlessly farther than the circumference of this earth;

it would wrap infinitely and eternally around and around this great planet. That's the true span of the life, the true length of the dash, for immortal souls made in the image of an immortal God.

I have little capacity to grasp eternity, to imagine forever, to understand what begins but never ends. My mind is too weak, my imagination too limited, my vision too clouded. Yet this is the promise God has made—that those who put their faith in Jesus receive life eternal, that those who accept his gift of grace are granted life unending, that those who die in him will reign with him forever and ever.

I am both challenged and comforted by this thought. I often lament the brevity of Nick's life, the abruptness of his departure. I often wonder what significance there can be in a life that was only twenty years long. But if our dashes extend endlessly into the infinite reaches of time and space, there is little difference between the one inch or two, between the two inches or four, that represent our time here on earth. This world is merely the place of preparation for what lies beyond. It is the classroom, the training ground, the finishing school. Even those who die the oldest are like a mist that appears for just a while and then vanishes, like a breath that is drawn in, held for a moment, and then released. Compared to the endless ages beyond, even the longest life here is the blink of an eye, the tick of a clock, the length of a dash.

When Jesus was preparing to say farewell to his disciples, he gave them a promise: "A little while, and you will see me no longer; and again a little while, and you will see me."[1] He was going away, but not permanently. He was departing, but not for good. "Just a little while," he assured them. That promise must have been precious to them as they waited in bewilderment following his crucifixion, as they waited in anticipation following his ascension, as they labored through persecution following Pentecost. "Just a little while." Just hold on a little longer. Just endure for a short time more. Just wait for a moment, for a tick, for a dash, and then you'll see that I'm true to my word, faithful to my every promise.

"Just a little while." These are words I am clinging to every bit as much as the disciples. I miss Nick more than I have the capacity to express. I ache to see him, long to hug him, yearn to talk with him. And I will. I'm sure I will. Jesus has promised there is boundless joy beyond this bounded life. I don't know how much time the Lord has allotted to me. I don't know when my "little while" will arrive, when my turn will come to be lowered into the ground beside my boy, when my gravestone will be ordered and carved and installed. I don't know what date will be etched onto its surface to represent the time of my departure. But I do know that, whether it is days from now or decades, the line between the day of my birth and the day of my death will represent a blip, just the briefest of moments, when compared to the vast eternity to come. And then I'll be forever with my boy, just beyond the edge of my dash.

CHAPTER 24

an empty room

We would have been clearing out Nick's room regardless. Had all gone according to plan—his plan and ours—he would be getting married in a few weeks and no longer need the bedroom that was his for almost twenty years. But things did not go according to plan—his plan or ours—and we are now clearing out his bedroom under very different circumstances.

It has taken us more than five months to get to this point. For five months, everything has been left almost exactly as it was when he walked out of this room to return to seminary for his junior year. For five months, it has been a kind of monument, a time capsule frozen in a moment, a reminder of happier days. For five months, the door has remained closed.

His room is one of the few things in this world that he truly made his own. Birds have their nests and foxes their holes and young men their bedrooms. He chose the pictures on the wall and bought the books on the shelves. The trinkets set here are the ones that were in some way important to him, and the letters collected over there are the ones his fiancée had sent while they endured a long winter's separation. It even somehow still smells like him in here, though I can't quite figure out how—perhaps it's the faded scent of his deodorant or hair gel. I understand why some parents can never bring themselves to change even the smallest detail of their child's room. To them it becomes a kind of shrine, a kind of sacred space, where they can go and reflect, go and remember, go and mourn.

There is something significant about beginning this process, about picking up that first item and carrying it out. It will be a kind of admission that Nick will never again need this space or anything in it. He will never spend another night in his bed, never play another game on his computer, never read another book from his shelves. It will somehow feel both rude and imposing—what right do we have to barge in and sort through his possessions? Who are we to decide what will be kept and what will be discarded, what will be treasured and what will be thrown away? Yet it must be done.

It must be done because we are practical people who live in a small house, and we know this will make a fine guest room. But Aileen insists we must begin afresh—everything must go and be replaced. There can be no link between the room as it was and the room as it will be—no common paint colors, no common furniture, no common pictures on the wall. It can be the same space, but it must be a new room.

We begin with the books. His childhood favorites are here—the adventure stories that so quickly gave way to works of history. I'm reminded of the time we made a long journey by plane and told him he could bring only two books.

He obediently packed just two—a history of Canada and a history of the Third Reich that between them had more than three thousand pages and weighed in at seven pounds. I think I'll keep those two. Nearby are his seminary textbooks—New Testament, Greek, Hebrew, preaching, counseling. I set aside his Greek New Testament, remembering a letter his professor sent to say that Nick was one of the best Greek students he had ever had.

The clothes are next to go, then the pictures, and then the bed. We will keep the mattress and the frame, but the blankets will have to be replaced. I notice the room is beginning to echo as it gets progressively emptier.

The desk is last to go. It sits in the far corner of the room, its surface bare, dusty, scratched. I can't help but think of all the times I knocked on Nick's door, listened until he said, "Come in!" then entered to see him sitting there, his face glowing by the light of the computer screen. As I walked in, he would tear his gaze from his document or his game, swivel his chair, prop his feet on the foot of the bed, and say, "What's up?" I still almost expect to find him, to see him, to hear him, whenever I enter.

And now his room is empty, no more than four bare walls and a faded parquet floor we somehow never got around to replacing. But his room is really no longer his room at all, is it? By clearing away his possessions, we have cleared away his claim to it. There is no longer a spot in the world that is his, no longer a room of his own, no longer a place he can return to. He has moved out and moved on.

Toronto is usually judged to be the most multicultural city

in the world, since every year, hundreds of thousands of people immigrate to it from all across the globe. Often, over the course of years and decades, entire extended families will make the journey. The younger people tend to come first, and then, as soon as they can, they fetch their spouses and children. Once the family has become established and has built up some wealth, they reach back across the ocean to extend the invitation to their parents, grandparents, or other relatives. As one family member after another makes the journey, the people remaining in India or Nigeria or the Philippines must feel their grip on their own countries begin to loosen. As they watch a growing number of their loved ones make the journey to that far country, as their homes become emptier and emptier, their loyalties must become divided. By the time their own paperwork has been cleared and they themselves are boarding a plane, they must feel every bit as much Canadian as they do Indian, Nigerian, or Filipino.

And standing here in this empty room, I can sense this same divided loyalty within my heart. Nick moved out of this room and out of this land to take up residence in one above, where my father, my aunt, and my grandmother had already taken up theirs. As time passes, I know that a greater number of my loved ones will make that same journey. Eventually, there may be more of them in heaven than on earth, more to draw me there than to hold me here. And soon enough, my paperwork will clear, and I, too, will be summoned across the ocean, summoned spiritually to that place my heart has already gone.[1]

But until then, an empty room awaits my attention. Tomorrow, Aileen will get out the paint and the brushes and begin to change the color of the walls. Next week, we will assemble new furniture, move it all in, and arrange it just right. The week after that, this room will be unrecognizable. We already know who will receive the first invitation to stay here. When Nick departed and left a fiancée behind, we assured his sweet Ryn that we would forever love her as the daughter she so nearly became, that we would be family to her for as long as she would allow us to be. "Let's call this 'Ryn's Room,'" I say to Aileen. "That way, our home will always be her home." And with that, we walk out, this time leaving the door wide open.

CHAPTER 25

how many children
do i have?

Some of my favorite anecdotes from the life of Jesus came in
those times when the religious authorities tried to trap him, to
expose him, to make him look like a rube. Despite their best and
repeated efforts, it never once ended well for them.

The Gospel of Mark describes a time when a group called
the Sadducees made their best attempt. The Sadducees believed
in no spirit, no angels, no reality beyond what could be seen
and touched. They certainly did not believe in a resurrection
of the dead. And so they crafted a little scenario meant to trap
Jesus and expose his ignorance when it came to life after death.
"Suppose a woman married seven times over the course of her
life," they said, "each one a legitimate marriage since it followed
the death of the previous husband. In the resurrection, whose
wife will she be, since she married all seven of them? Tell us that,
if you know so much!"

Jesus' response showcased their ignorance: "The mistake

you've made," he told them, "is that you don't know the Bible and you don't know the power of God. Blinded by your ignorance, you have overlooked the unmistakably clear message of the Scriptures. If you're so knowledgeable about all that they say, how is it that you've never noticed the simplest of details: When God appeared to Moses from the burning bush, he introduced himself by saying, 'I am the God of Abraham, the God of Isaac, and the God of Jacob.' He didn't say, 'I *was* their God,' but 'I *am* their God.' Surely you can see it: he is not God of the dead, but of the living." It was the ultimate mic drop moment long before there were mics to drop, and through it, Jesus provided assurance that there is, indeed, life that follows death.[1]

I have been thinking of Jesus' response as I face a question that is, on the face of it, perfectly simple: How many children do I have? It should be perfectly simple and once was, but I am now finding it rather complicated, for it intersects matters that span life and death, earth and heaven, time and eternity.

A publisher recently got in touch to remind me that I submitted a manuscript to them several months ago. In the meantime, they have edited the words, designed the cover, and laid out the text. The last thing they need before they send it all to the printer is my brief biography for the back cover.[2]

For many years, that little bio has said something like this: "Tim Challies is a Christian, a husband to Aileen, and a father to three children. He worships and serves as an elder at Grace Fellowship Church in Toronto, Ontario." That line about "a father to three children" has been incrementally modified over the years. It progressed from "a father to three young children" to "a father to three teenaged children" to "a father to three children in their teens and twenties." It has changed with the changing circumstances of my life.

And now I realize it will need to change again. But how? Am I still a father to three children? Or am I now a father to only two? Would it not be disloyal to Nick's memory to erase him from my little biography as if he had never existed at all? Yet acknowledging him will inevitably lead to the kind of awkwardness I experienced at the bank the other day when an account manager made some polite small talk about family, and I said I had three children, and he pressed deeper, and I had to explain that one of them had died. He blushed, I cringed, the small talk sputtered out.

So how many children do I have? I've decided that for now, very pragmatically, I will sometimes answer two and sometimes three, depending on the circumstance. When I'm in a casual conversation with someone who is merely engaging in polite banter, I'll probably just say two. That's true enough for the context. But when I'm in more formal conversation or providing a bio for the back cover of a book, I will answer in a way that's truer still: I am a father to three children. For if, in keeping with Jesus' response to the Sadducees, God makes no distinction between his children who are in heaven and his children who are on earth, then neither will I. If God is God to Abraham, Isaac, and Jacob, then surely I am no less father to Michaela, Abby, and Nick.

Just as Nick *was* my son and I *was* Nick's father, Nick *is* my son and I *am* his father. Better still, he always *will be* my son and I always *will be* his father. I was, am, and forever will be as much a father to him as to his sisters. There is no context in time or eternity that can change that. And so, on the back of that book, you'll read "Tim Challies is a Christian, a husband to Aileen, and a father to two girls in their teens and one son who is waiting for him in heaven." I am not a father of the dead, but of the living—the two living here with me and the one living there with God.

CHAPTER 26

the cause of death

Why did the *Titanic* sink? Was it because the ship struck an iceberg? Or was it because it had been poorly built, because the captain was reckless, because the lookout failed in his duty? Why did the First World War begin? Was it because of the assassination of Archduke Franz Ferdinand? Or was it because of the crumbling of an old world order, because of a network of secret alliances, because of the rise of nationalist pride? Why did Jesus die? Was it because of the demands of the religious authorities? Or was it because of the cowardice of Pilate, because of the persecution of the Roman Empire, because God willed it? None of these answers are wrong, but none of these answers are complete, for any one event can have many causes.

For months, I have been wondering how Nick died. I already knew the basics, of course—he collapsed while playing a game and was found to have neither heartbeat nor respiration. His friends could not revive him and neither could a passing doctor, an ambulance crew, or an emergency room team. While I have known the basics of what happened, I haven't known the cause. But today, finally, I have received a nondescript, hand-written envelope marked "Jefferson County Coroner's Office."

I know better than to read the autopsy report. Not only will it contain medical jargon that is beyond my comprehension, but of much greater concern, it will contain descriptive details that will trigger my imagination and burden my soul. A doctor friend has read many such reports and has kindly offered to read and summarize it on my behalf. I open the envelope to find six single-sided, typewritten pages. I quickly snap a photo of each one of them, doing my best to keep my eyes from focusing on as much as a single word. With that task done, I stuff the report into a fresh envelope, seal it, and bury it at the bottom of my document safe. I'll be glad if I never see it again.

As I wait for my friend to read it and report back, I can't help but ponder, *What was the cause of Nick's death?*

I know there is an answer that addresses the basic physiology of the matter. Our bodies are intricately made, wonderfully woven together, created to thrive on this planet in its oxygen-rich atmosphere. The most basic cause of death for any of us is being deprived of that precious oxygen, for when it can no longer nourish our bodies, the tissues quickly succumb. I know that, in some way and for some reason, Nick's organs were deprived of oxygen for so long that the damage became too extensive for him to survive. In this way, the cause of his death was a lack of oxygen.

But then there is another answer, one that approaches the matter from a spiritual angle to tell me that the cause of death was sin—not necessarily any sin Nick committed, but its very existence in this world. After all, this world was created free from depravity and therefore free from death. Yet God clearly warned humanity that if they chose to defy his ways, they would die. Had the first human beings remained faithful, neither sin nor death would ever have made an appearance. But they failed to obey God, and as they embraced temptation, death began its reign. Sin claimed Nick's life.

And then closely connected to this answer is one that acknowledges the existence of a tempter—one who was active in leading those first human beings astray. Satan is the father of lies, the one who convinced Adam and Eve to believe that God had been deceptive, that he had withheld something from them that would be for their benefit rather than their harm. By leading them to sin, he led them to their grave. And in that way, Satan lurks in the background of Nick's death.

But most important of all is the answer of providence, which considers God's involvement. God makes it clear that he is the one who begins life and ends life, who raises up and brings back down.[1] The Lord is the one who gives and who takes away, so that each of us is born according to the will of God and dies according to the will of God. There is no one who can die before God's appointed time and no one who can remain alive after it. There is no tragedy that can claim us before the hour God has ordained and no miracle that can save us after it. God and God alone has ultimate authority over life and death. Simply put, Nick could not have died had it not been God's will. In the most ultimate sense, Nick's cause of death is God himself.

Yet God uses means to carry out his providence, and that

is what I have waited so long to know. And now my friend is calling to tell me the specific means God used to call Nick from life to death, from earth to heaven. Though the coroner cannot be completely certain, the evidence seems to indicate a cardiac dysrhythmia. For reasons that are likely to remain forever unknown, Nick's heart began to beat in an erratic rhythm—and one that quickly led to full cardiac arrest. He immediately fell unconscious and dropped to the ground. Since the equipment needed to restart his heart was not available, he died.

And now I know. It is an answer that is both comforting and terrifying. It is comforting to know Nick did not linger and did not suffer. It is comforting to know there was nothing we should have spotted and nothing we could have known. It is comforting to know it's not his fault, not our fault, and not the fault of his friends who tried so hard to save him. We will be sure to relieve them of the burden they've been carrying.

But it is terrifying as well, for it shows the magnitude of the power of God and his willingness to exercise it. Conversely, it shows the frailty of humanity and our utter dependence on divine providence. A few chaotic electrical impulses were all it took to stop an otherwise healthy heart and interrupt an otherwise normal life. "Our God is in the heavens; he does all that he pleases."[2] He does, indeed, for he was pleased to very suddenly and decisively reach into my comfortable life and take my son. He gave no warning. He offered no explanation. He made no apology. He just reached out and took what was so precious. He just reached out, called Nick home, and left me bereaved.

But I cannot hold it against him. I cannot charge him with

wrong, for he is the one who begins every life, the one who has authority over every life, and the one who ultimately ends every life. That is true, whether the end comes at twenty or at eighty, in a park or in a hospital, in a way that was predicted or one that was entirely unexpected. Our lives are not our own. They never are. They never were. "In *his* hand is the life of every living thing and the breath of all mankind."[3]

And so God has done no more than exercise his lawful prerogative. The only fitting response is to bow before him, to submit to his authority, and to trust that he does all things well. For while his arm is strong, his mind is vast, his heart is kind, his love is true, and his purpose is good. I believe and profess there is nothing better than for God to do whatever he pleases, nothing more suitable than for God to work his will. That is true, whether it leads to laughter or tears, whether it brings me pleasure or pain, whether it gives or takes away.

CHAPTER 27

the trumpet
shall sound

It has become my custom to visit Nick on Sunday afternoons. I eat my lunch and then, before settling in with a book or a ball game, make the short drive to the cemetery. It's a tradition I've come to treasure because it's on that little patch of tear-soaked ground, there before that slab of dark stone, that I feel closest to him. In all the earth, it feels like the nearest point of contact between father and son. I cannot see him, I cannot speak with him, I cannot wrap my arms around him, but I can, at least, be there.

Today I have chosen to come early, to come before dawn, to come and watch the sun rise, for this Sunday is Easter Sunday. The ground is frosted white and the air is cool. It is, after all, still only early April here in Canada. The sky is beginning to reflect the first rays of the rising sun, and I find myself wondering, *How far away are the dead from the living? What separates our dearly departed from we who remain? Is it a chasm or is it a ditch? Is it a moment or an age? Is it a partition of paper or a citadel of stone? Is it a deep sea that stretches beyond the horizon or a shallow puddle that evaporates beneath our feet? How near or how far am I from my boy?*

I put my headphones on, open my music app, and select Handel's *Messiah*, the soundtrack to so many of my life's greatest joys and deepest sorrows. I advance to the third part, the second scene, the forty-seventh movement, and listen as the bass soloist begins to sing, "Behold, I tell you a mystery, we shall not all sleep, but we shall all be changed, in a moment, in the twinkling of an eye, at the last trumpet."[1] This is Scripture set to music, truth wrapped in oratorio.

A well-meaning friend once brought a word meant to console: Nick has become a star shining in the night sky, smiling down on you. But I know souls are souls and stars are stars, and ne'er the twain shall meet, for they are of a different substance. A soul can no more become a star than a star can become a soul. Still I wonder, *Is he nearer or farther than the distance between that star and this earth?*

Another friend said Nick has joined the ranks of the angels and is more present with us now than he has ever been. But as stars are stars and souls are souls, angels are angels and human beings are human beings. God created both, but with distinction. Surely Nick has not exchanged his humanity for something of an entirely different order. Still I wonder, *Is he nearer or farther than the distance between human beings and angels, between the world that is visible and the world that is veiled to our eyes?*

A gentle gust of wind stirs the young tree that stands to the side of his grave, its first buds just beginning to form in the warming spring weather. The music advances to the next track, and I hear the soloist begin to sing, "The trumpet shall sound and the dead shall be raised incorruptible, and we shall be changed." Something now stirs inside my heart. *How close is Nick?*

I see it now. Better said, I hear it. He is not far—not far at all. He is just one trumpet blast away, for as I've just heard, the end will begin with a piercing blast to announce the coming of the King, to wake the slumbering dead. But there's more. Nick is just one great shout away, for Jesus "will descend from heaven with a cry of command, with the voice of an archangel."[2] In one moment, all will be still, and in the next, the world will resound with a mighty cry that will shake the earth and split the skies. Perhaps best of all, Nick is just one moment away, for Christ has promised to return suddenly—"in a moment, in the twinkling of an eye."[3] It could be now. Or now. Or now. "As the lightning flashes and lights up the sky from one side to the other, so will the Son of Man be in his day."[4] Thousands of years of history will be consummated in that single moment.

I hear the countertenor take over from the bass. "Then shall be brought to pass the saying that is written: 'Death is swallowed up in victory.'" Then, in that very moment, at the sound of the trumpet and the cry of command, death's reign will come to an end. Then, in that moment, this cemetery, this place of my greatest sorrow, will become the place of my greatest joy, for this ground will give up her dead. They will rise—this one, that one, all who love God—together rising to meet the Lord. This place where we do the most unnatural thing—lower bodies into the cold ground—will be the place we witness the most incredible thing—bodies being raised from the ground to never die again.

The tenor joins the countertenor to begin a duet, and they sing together, "O death, where is thy sting?" The choir takes over: "But thanks be to God, who giveth us the victory through our Lord Jesus Christ." Death has lost its sting because death has been defeated by the resurrection of Jesus Christ. What seemed to be a great defeat on Friday was turned into a great triumph on Sunday! Easter is the day of resurrection, the day of victory, the day of hope.

And now that hope swells within as *Messiah* comes to its great crescendo. Though Handel's masterpiece is known for its famous "Hallelujah" chorus, I have always preferred this final chorus, for in it the choir joins the saints and the martyrs, the living creatures and the elders, to sing together, "Worthy is the Lamb that was slain, and hath redeemed us to God by his blood, to receive power, and riches, and wisdom, and strength, and honour, and glory, and blessing." This choir joins with every creature in heaven and on earth and under the earth and in the sea to sing, "Blessing and honour, glory and power, be unto him that sitteth upon the throne, and unto the Lamb, for ever and ever." They echo the four living creatures in Revelation as they cry out, "Amen." Again and again, through hundreds of repetitions, then thousands, the choir repeats that precious word. "Amen"—it is true and certain, it will come to be, for God has decreed it. And so, "Amen," I say. Joining the elders, I fall before the throne, before the King, and worship his name with a loud "amen."

CHAPTER 28

follow in my footsteps

High in the mountains of Switzerland we came to a part of the trail that passed along a ridge, a narrow edge that divided two sides of a towering mountain. The way was wide where we stood and wide farther ahead, but to get from this point to the other we would need to follow a small, winding trail that was slick with morning dew and had sheer slopes beside it plummeting away to deep valleys. Nick never did well with heights, never saw much benefit in taking unnecessary risks. His eyes were wide, his face pale, his feet frozen in place. I turned back and stood with him a moment, attempting to comfort and reassure him. "Just follow in my footsteps," I said. "Don't be afraid. Match your steps to mine and I'll lead you across."

Such is the calling of a father in small moments like this as well as ones far more consequential—to lead the way his children will follow. And while this is his duty toward all of his children, it is particularly true for his sons, for as a mother bears a special responsibility to mentor her girls, so a father does for his boys. A father is meant to live in such a way that he can tell his sons, sometimes literally and sometimes figuratively, "Just follow in my footsteps." "Do you need to know how to live as a Christian in this world? Follow in my footsteps. Do you need to know how to work hard at your vocation? Follow in my footsteps. Do you need to know how to love a wife and lead a family? Follow in my footsteps."

I loved leading Nick. I loved to see him beginning to follow me, imitating me as I did my best to imitate Christ. I saw him adopt some of my best habits, mimic some of my best traits. I saw him study the way I related to his mother, scrutinize the way I related to the people I've been called to pastor. I took seriously my responsibility to lead and he took seriously his responsibility to follow.

I assumed I would lead Nick for longer than I did. I assumed I would lead him into marriage and ministry and fatherhood. I assumed I would lead him all the way through life and all the way to glory. I assumed that as he prepared to cross that narrow ridge that leads between two worlds, he would be able to put his feet where mine had already passed, just as he did on that pathway between two alpine plateaus.

That's not to say I was quite ready to lead that particular way. As Nick was afraid to pass along a Swiss mountain ridge with sheer slopes to either side of it, I was afraid to pass along the narrow way that leads from life to death. I was afraid to die. I knew Jesus had already led the way, that we are to merely follow in the path he first trod. As God led his people through the night with light blazing from a pillar of fire, we are led through death by the One who is the very light of life.[1] But the thought still frightened me. I still wasn't able to trust, still wasn't ready to go.

At Nick's funeral I asked that we sing the old hymn "Face to Face" so we could profess together our confidence that each of us will someday stand before the face of Christ himself.

> Face to face—oh, blissful moment!
> Face to face—to see and know;
> Face to face with my Redeemer,
> Jesus Christ who loves me so.[2]

But I can't deny that I have often looked forward to that day and feared that day with equal measure. I have wanted to be with Christ, but I've been loath to be away from all that is here. I have longed to be face-to-face with him, but I've been afraid to leave the familiarity of this world for the uncertainty of the next. I've sometimes preferred earth to heaven, sight to faith, here to there.

But then Nick leapfrogged me on the way. The follower became the leader, and the leader the follower. And in surging on ahead of me, he has given me heart, he has given me faith, he has given me courage. My fear of death evaporated in the moment of Nick's. Why should I be afraid to walk in the way he has already gone? How could my courage fail when his held fast? Knowing he will not return to me, why should I be the least bit afraid to go to him?

But there is one matter that perplexes me, one detail that concerns me. In my thoughts of heaven, Nick has as much prominence as Jesus. If I'm honest, he often has more. Jesus promised he would go ahead and prepare a place for us, that where he is, we could be as well. But where he is, is where Nick is, and I cannot easily separate the two. To be in heaven is to be at home with the Lord, said Paul.[3] But it's also to be at home with Nick. What does it say about me that my longing to be with Jesus is now matched, or even surpassed, by my longing to be with Nick?

In the early days, when the grief was still so present, still so overwhelming, still so raw, I confessed this to a friend: "When my thoughts turn to heaven, I'm thinking less of meeting Jesus and more of seeing Nick. I'm eager to see my Savior but aching to see my boy. I must sound like an absolute pagan."

"No," he replied gently, "You sound like a grieving father."

And I'm content to leave it there. It was God who called me to himself and God who put a great love for himself in my heart. It was God who gave me my son, God who gave me such love for him, and God who took him away from me. The Lord knows I love the Lord, and the Lord knows I love my boy. I'll leave it to him to sort out the details.

In the meantime, I'm ready to die, ready to walk the narrow ridge that leads from here to there. That's not to say I have given up on life and actually want to die or will do anything to hasten it. I still have people to live for, still have duties to perform, still have callings to fulfill. I'm content to stay here until the Lord beckons me home. But when he does, I'll jump to my feet and race that ridge without a fear in the world. I'm ready to follow joyfully, courageously, confidently in the footsteps of a Savior, and a son, who have already led the way.

CHAPTER 29

the sacred circle

The Prince of Preachers has slapped me across the face. Reaching through the 130 years that separate us, Charles Spurgeon has confronted and rebuked me. He has spoken words that have brought a challenge to the midst of my sorrow, a reprimand to the depths of my despair. Moses needed his Jethro, Peter his Paul, Calvin his Farel, and I my Charles. This is a hard message he has brought me, but one I needed to hear.

"The singularity of sorrow is a dream of the sufferer," he says.[1] Here in an especially dark moment on an especially difficult day, I am tempted to think that my suffering is utterly unique, that I and I alone have now faced the worst this world can bring. I find myself tempted to compare the loss of a twenty-year-old son—an only and firstborn son—to every other kind of loss and to determine that none could be harder. But Spurgeon calls me out: "Thou sittest alone and keepest silence, and thou sayest in thy heart, '*I* am the man that hath seen affliction.'" This is exactly my temptation—to think that no one has seen affliction like I have, to content myself that no one can sympathize with me because no one has suffered like me.

But there must be a "but," and sure enough, Spurgeon provides one: "But a host of others have seen affliction as well as thyself." The reality is that I am not alone in my suffering and I have not been dealt a harsher blow than so many others. And so in love he confronts me. In love he says, "Come down from thine elevation of special woo; indulge no longer the egotism of despair. Thou art but one pilgrim along the well-trodden Via Dolorosa." And in a moment I feel like I have been awakened, for I know that he is right. "Thou art the man," said Nathan to David.[2] And "thou art the man," says Charles to me.

Now with fresh eyes I gaze toward that way of sorrow, that pathway of suffering, and I see that "the stair-way of grief is never without its passengers, and at their head is he whose name is 'A man of sorrows and acquainted with grief.'" In the great company of saints are many who know my loss, many who carry a great burden, many who walk with a pronounced limp. And at the head of us all is the bent and broken form of a man carrying a heavy cross.

I squint my eyes to see who walks the way before me, and familiar faces soon begin to materialize—faces I know from the pages of Scripture and the annals of history. The Bible is only four chapters into its grand narrative when the first death strikes the first parents and the hearts of Adam and Eve are broken by the death of Abel. Not long afterward, Job suffers the loss of no fewer than ten of his children—seven sons and three daughters. Aaron's sons Nadab and Abihu soon fall before God's judgment, while Eli's Hophni and Phinehas fall before the enemy. Naomi is grieving the loss of her husband when her sorrow is compounded by the death of her sons Mahlon and Chilion. Just a few generations later, David suffers first the loss of his infant son and then of his favored son. As the Old Testament gives way to the New, Zechariah and Elizabeth grieve the loss of John at the hand of Herod, while Mary grieves the loss of Jesus at the hand of Pilate.

As history carries on and the ranks of the faithful continue to march past me, I spot the tearstained faces of many more dear saints who know what it is to lose a child. Katharina von Bora bore Martin Luther six children, one of whom died in infancy, while another, their precious Magdalena, died in her father's arms at the age of just thirteen. Idelette Calvin bore John only one child, a son named Jacques, but he was born prematurely and survived only briefly. John Owen had eleven children, only one of whom survived to adulthood, and even that one daughter still died before her father. John Bunyan suffered a grievous blow when he lost his precious Mary, who had cared for him so tenderly during his long imprisonment. God filled Cotton Mather's quiver, but death emptied it, for Mather outlived only two of his fifteen children.

As the death of a child touched Reformers and Puritans, so too were the great poets affected by loss, many of whom used their craft to express their grief. Charles Wesley lamented a son in "Wherefore Should I Make My Moan":

> God forbids his longer stay;
> God recalls the precious loan;

God hath taken him away,
From my bosom to His own:
Surely what He wills is best:
Happy in His will I rest.[3]

Henry Wadsworth Longfellow mourned a daughter in "Resignation":

Not as a child shall we again behold her;
For when with raptures wild
In our embraces we again enfold her,
She will not be a child;

But a fair maiden, in her Father's mansion,
Clothed with celestial grace;
And beautiful with all the soul's expansion
Shall we behold her face.[4]

Hannah Flagg Gould wrote of a child who had lived but a year and a day:

To grief the night-hours keeping,
A mournful mother lay
Upon her pillow, weeping—
Her babe had passed away.

When she had clasped her treasure
A year and yet a day,

Of time 't was all its measure—
'T was gone, like morning's ray![5]

John Paton was just three months into his ministry among the cannibalistic tribes of the New Hebrides when his son was born, yet within days of the happy occasion, both his wife and child would be laid in the grave. David and Mary Livingstone lost a daughter, William and Dorothy Carey two daughters and a son, Hudson and Maria Taylor four of their eight children before they even reached the age of ten.

Fanny Crosby spoke of her bereavement only to say, "God gave us a tender babe but the angels came down and took our infant up to God and to His throne."[6] Theodore Cuyler, at one time pastor of the largest Presbyterian Church in the United States, lost two of his children in infancy and another at twenty-one, and often wrote movingly of his visits to Green-Wood Cemetery where they, and now he, await the day of resurrection. His southern contemporary, Thomas Smyth, laid two young children in the very same grave on the very same day.

Time would fail me to tell of Matthew Henry, Jonathan Edwards, George Whitefield, Lemuel Haynes, Selina Hastings, Frederick Douglass, George Müller, and so many others.[7] It would fail me to tell of Charles Spurgeon and D. L. Moody and so many others who endured the double sorrow of the loss of a grandchild. It is only in the most modern of times and the most privileged of nations that the death of children takes us by surprise and strikes us as unusual. Spurgeon is exactly right when he says that the singularity of sorrow is but a dream of the one who suffers. A host of precious brothers and sisters can sympathize with my loss, for they have suffered it themselves. Their suffering has equipped them to commiserate, to comfort me in my sorrow.[8] I feel them drawing alongside me. I do not walk alone.

And it isn't just the dead who come to me, but also the living. Just days after Nick goes to Jesus, a grieving father who lives far away reaches out with a long letter to share his experience from the death of his twenty-year-old son. It becomes my manual, my guidebook, through those earliest days. A mutual friend connects us to a couple who lives just a town over and who lost a son ten years before. Aileen and I meet with them, speak with them, weep with them, and are blessed by their friendship and prayers. A pastor who reads my early articles about Nick and thinks, *I can't imagine what that would be like*, suffers the loss of his young son exactly one month later. He and his wife soon become friends. With such people we can talk freely, honestly, knowingly, for we are walking the same road.

It is in the pages of one of Theodore Cuyler's books that I find a comforting phrase. Following the death of his young Georgie, he had received an outpouring of correspondence as so many friends, readers, and parishioners wrote with words of comfort and consolation. He soon came to realize, as have I, that the death of a child had ushered him into "the sacred circle of the sorrowing," a community made up of fellow sufferers. He had not been invited into the circle or asked if he wished to join. Rather, Providence had directed him to be part of it, and he had chosen to submit, to bow the knee.[9]

I would never wish it on anyone to join this circle, this club, for the membership fee is the death of a child and the dues are a broken heart. Yet priceless consolation comes to those who have joined, for we know that none of us need ever stand alone. Even if we have no one in our family, neighborhood, or church who has suffered such a loss, in this circle we join with those who have gone before through their sermons and books, their poems and songs. We join in fellowship with them so they can commiserate with us, encourage us, and cheer us on. Through the millennia, we clasp the hands of our fellow mourners as we stand and grieve together, as we spur one another on to love and good deeds, as we approach that place where God himself will wipe away every tear from our eyes, where death shall be no more, and where there shall there be no more mourning, no more crying, and no more pain, for these former things will have fully and finally passed away.[10]

angels unaware

It's too much today. It's too heavy, too sad, too sorrowful. I'm drowning. I'm overwhelmed. I'm going under. I need an angel to come and minister to me in this garden of grief, an Aaron to hold my arms through this long battle, a Jonathan to strengthen me in God. I need a shepherd's staff to pull me close, a father's arms to hold me tight, a bird's wings to shelter me safe. I need something. Please, God, give me something.

I thought this would be easier by now. I thought I would have come farther. But today is the day Nick had planned to be married, and the sorrow of it has snuck up on me and caught me unawares. Fresh waves of grief are washing over me as I ponder what should have been or at least what could have been. This day could have been among my all-time highs but is instead among my all-time lows. It could have been a day of great celebration but is instead a day of the deepest sadness. I've mourned what was, but today I mourn what will never be.

Aileen comes downstairs to rouse me from my despondency so we can head to the cemetery. We deviate from our usual route to stop at a local florist, who has prepared a boutonniere of just the kind Nick would have pinned to his suit today. One white rose, sage green leaves, little sprigs of baby's breath. I picture him in my mind—tall, proud, eager, nervous. He would have looked so handsome. We drive in silence, our tears saying what our mouths cannot.

The cemetery is quiet this morning, and it looks like we have the place nearly to ourselves, save for a gardener tending the grass far in the distance. We lay the boutonniere by the grave, and I place a cup of coffee beside it—little gifts from us to him. In my pocket I have a bundle of papers, the speech I would have delivered at his wedding reception. I have written it for my sake more than his, of course. But even though he can't hear, I still want to say all the things a father would say at his son's wedding. I want to express my joy, my love, my pride. I had planned to stand here and say it all aloud, but now that it comes to it, I find that I don't have the strength, I don't have the words, I don't have the voice. So I fold it up carefully and nestle it tenderly in the shadow of his gravestone. It will have to remain unread.

For a time, we simply stand in silence and gaze at it all, side by side, arm in arm. Together we weep, a brokenhearted father and brokenhearted mother drowning in our grief. We are dejected. We are lonely. We are abandoned. *My God, my God, why?*

The silence is broken as a voice speaks my name. We turn around to see that a man and woman have approached us from behind. They introduce themselves as fellow Christians who are familiar with my website and who have been reading my articles and family updates. They tell us that their son is buried just a few rows over from Nick and that they are just a little further along the road of grief than we are. Though it is not their custom to visit the cemetery on Saturdays, they felt led to do so on this particular day and at this particular time. They saw us and recognized us, and they made their way over.

We try to speak to these kind folks—we *want* to speak to them—but the words catch in our throats. There is so much we'd like to say, but the words don't come. Grief has rendered us mute.

They see our tears, they hear our sorrow, and they understand. They say those precious words, "Let's pray together." They pray wonderfully, beautifully, passionately. They pray as people who know God as a friend knows a friend. They pray as people who know what it is to be bereaved, who know what it is to be brokenhearted, who know what it is to cry out from the depths of their souls. They pray down heaven's comfort until it falls on us like the warm rays of the afternoon sun.

As they take their leave, I can scarcely believe how God has provided. He heard the cry of our hearts, and he sent his angels. He knew our need, and he dispatched his messengers. And it strikes me that the tears now cascading from my eyes have become tears of joy, tears of gratitude, tears of praise. "I have been young, and now am old," said David, "yet I have not seen the righteous forsaken."[1] I should have known. I should have believed.

Now, with the strength God has provided, I can read the speech I prepared for my boy, the speech that was meant to be delivered in the hustle and bustle of a reception hall but must now be delivered in the solitude of a cemetery. I imagine Nick in his suit, Ryn in her dress, my girls as bridesmaids, Aileen glowing with pride. And I read:

> I suppose every parent can attest that it's not just a bride who dreams of her wedding day, and not just a groom who dreams of his, but their parents as well. So this is a day Aileen and I have dreamed about, a day we have prayed toward. This is a day of such joy, such anticipation, such celebration.
>
> Nick, when you were tiny, no more than a few days old, I began to pray for your future spouse. I began to pray that God would set aside a wonderful, godly woman just for you—that he would first call her to himself and that he would then lead her to you. I prayed that prayer when you were a tiny baby in my arms, when you were a little child toddling about the house, when you were a gawky teenager heading out the door to high school, and when you were a scared young man we were leaving behind at college. It was not long after you arrived at Boyce that we began to hear the name Ryn. And after you dealt with some early rejection— and I'd even say well-deserved rejection for coming on just a little too fast and a little too strong—you caught your bearings, you regained your confidence, and you found your wife. And so this day is an answer to so many prayers.

And what a delight it has been to get to know your bride. Mom and I always knew you would pursue a woman of character, a woman who loved God and the people created in his image. And truly you outdid yourself. Ryn, we often wondered what it would be like to welcome another daughter into our family, but we couldn't have imagined how easy you would make it and what joy you would bring. We couldn't have imagined how quickly you'd become one of the girls—our girls. We're humbled that you'd be willing to join our family and take on our name. We're thankful that you're willing to dedicate your life to our son, even as he dedicates his life to you. You have gained yourself a husband who I can honestly say is one of the finest men I know. He is patient and kind. He is dutiful and honorable. He is slow to sin and quick to apologize. His giftings are many and his shortcomings are few. I'm so excited that you two have chosen to build a life together.

Nick, Solomon says, "A wise son brings joy to his father,"[2] and I can truly say that among all the many joys God has granted me in this life, few have been greater than the joy of being your dad. Few pleasures have blessed me more than watching you grow in wisdom and in godliness and in favor with God and man.[3] I'm thrilled to see the man you have become and the man you are becoming. I'm thrilled to see the ways you've grown in distinctly Christian character. I'm thrilled to see you work so hard to get a strong start in ministry and to prepare yourself for a lifetime of service to others. I'm so very proud of you. One of my highest honors is considering you not only a son but also a friend, not only a protégé but also a mentor. "He who loves wisdom makes his father glad."[4] And truly, my boy, you make my heart overflow with gladness, with joy, with pride.

At this point, I think I'm supposed to offer some words of counsel, some words of wisdom born from nearly a quarter-century of being married. So here goes. Treat each day as its own little life. Each morning marks the creation of a new day, and each evening marks its passing away. We cannot live in the past, and we cannot live in the future. We can only ever live in the day God has created for us. The key to living life well is to live each day well. So begin each day as a fresh opportunity to bring glory to God, and close each day as if you will never see another. Let no sin linger from one day to the next, no bitterness put down roots in the night. Let no promise remain unfulfilled, and withhold no good from the other when it is in your power to do it. If there are duties to be done, do them today, and if there are praises to be offered, offer them today. If there are sins to be confessed, confess them today, and if there are amends to be made, make them today. Yesterday is in the past and tomorrow is never guaranteed. There is only ever today.

And speaking of today, today is the day to celebrate you and to celebrate your marriage. Instead of closing with a traditional toast, I'd like to close with a biblical blessing, with the words of God himself: "Now may the God of peace himself sanctify you completely, and may your whole spirit and soul and body be kept blameless at the coming of our Lord Jesus Christ. He who calls you is faithful; he will surely do it. The grace of our Lord Jesus Christ be with you.[5] Amen."

We know that this very grace was with Nick in his life and in his death. And the same God who was so faithful to Nick has today proven his faithfulness to us. He has not left us. He has not forsaken us. He never would. He never will.

on the other side
of the wall

A story is told of a convalescent woman and the lovely vine that grew in her yard. Confined to her property during her long recovery from an accident, she turned her attention to the little plot of ground behind her home. She planted the vine on a cool spring morning, dreaming of the day when, given enough time and care, it would grow to cover the wall that marked the boundary of her property.

The woman loved her plant and tended to it conscientiously, pruning it, watering it, nourishing it. Under her care it took root and grew steadily, always reaching, always grasping, always clinging, as it spread both upward and outward. Before many seasons had passed, it covered her wall with its lush green leaves. But, despite her best efforts, it produced blossoms that were very tiny and very few. Nevertheless, she found in her plant a source of great wonder and true delight.

And so did the townsfolk, for unbeknownst to her, the

roots had pressed beneath the foundation of the wall; the branches had pushed through its cracks; and the tendrils had reached up and over its top where they spilled over the far side in a wondrous cascade of beautiful, fragrant flowers. Many people as they passed by paused to admire their beauty. Visiting friends described the scene to her and explained that the plant must prefer the far side of the wall, for where her yard was shadowed by the boughs of mighty oaks and elms, the other side was unshaded; where her yard caught only the cool morning light, the other side was exposed to the full heat of the afternoon sun. It was there, on the far side, that the blooms were biggest and loveliest, most fragrant and most vibrant.

She paused to consider these reports that her flowers were thriving on the far side of the wall. Should she lament that she could not see the best of their beauty, that others would enjoy them in a way she could not? She determined she would utter no complaint. She would rejoice in the beauty of her flowers, though she could not see them. She would find joy in the delight of the friends and strangers who crowded around them. And she anticipated the day when, healed and whole, she could at last pass through the garden gate and see them for herself.[1]

Like all fathers, I had hopes for my son but quickly learned that it was best to allow him to dream his own dreams, then to support him in the directions he chose. He came to dream of a simple, quiet life dedicated to family and the local church. And he set out to realize that ambition. He began to identify his gifts and to prepare himself to deploy them for the good of others and the glory of God. He began to hone talents and develop skills that would equip him for a lifetime of pastoral ministry. He began to sharpen his character, to advance in wisdom and stature and in favor with God and man.[2] He was making steady progress; he was on all the right trajectories. And then he was gone. He was gone before I could see him realize any of his dreams. He died a fiancé, not a husband; a student, not a graduate; an intern, not a pastor. He died before we could see him as a married man, a proud father, an ordained minister of the gospel. There was so much he left undone, so many beginnings and so few ends.

So what has become of all those dreams and ambitions? What has become of all that progress and advancement? What has become of his characteristic kindness and his disposition toward gentleness? What of his desire to serve God by serving others? Did it all pass away with him?

Surely not. Is it not likely that such noble dreams and ambitions, such rare and precious traits, are even more at home in heaven than on earth? Is it not plausible that in that place of perfection, they have not been erased but rather increased, not diminished but multiplied? Is it not appropriate, then, that I should turn my lamentation into praise, my grief into hope, my sorrow into expectation, confident that Nick has gone where he can thrive, where he can flourish, where his every dream can be made good? For though I cannot now see him, I can be certain he is blooming there, on the other side of the wall, where the sun is brighter, where all shadows are gone. And I can anticipate the day when I, too, will pass through the garden gate to finally see him in that place where he has gone not to die but to truly live.[3]

summer

CHAPTER 32

courage, dear heart

Though summer has only barely begun, we are in the midst of a long and scorching heat wave, already under drought conditions. This is usually a time of year when we can count on our lawns and gardens being at their full glory, but already the grass is beginning to look brown and dry, the flowers withered and faded. Southern Ontario is known for experiencing four distinct seasons that are roughly equal in length, but this year, the cool beauty of spring has too quickly faded into the full heat of summer.

A few weeks ago, the cemetery laid fresh sod over Nick's grave, a gentle green blanket to cover his final place of rest. But while it is their responsibility to lay the sod, they take little responsibility for watering it. Knowing that under these conditions it cannot last for long without a daily drenching, most evenings Aileen and I make the short drive to the cemetery. There we lug watering cans from the tap in the parking area down the long row of graves until we come at last to his. Back and forth we go, a few gallons at a time. The cracked, parched ground thirstily absorbs every drop, but the sod, at least, is thriving.

I have noticed that when I fill the big watering cans and set out toward Nick's grave, the load feels light in my hands. But as I continue on my way, treading the uneven ground between the roadway and his little plot, my arms begin to grow weary. By the time I draw close, my steps have grown heavy and my arms have begun to ache. I often need to take a little breather before I can pour out the water and then repeat the trip again. In its own way, this process strikes me as a parable for the journey of grief.

I sometimes think back to those early days when grief was still a stranger we were just getting to know. It was a grueling stretch of time marked by shock, uncertainty, and deep heartbreak. I would not wish it upon my worst enemy. Yet while those days were hard, they were also simpler. We had little time to think, little time to ponder, little time to wrestle. We had a million decisions we had to make, a million actions we had to take. We were overwhelmed by offers of help, deluged with shows of support and messages of sympathy. The first days and weeks passed in a kind of blur, a frenetic whirlwind of activity.

Eventually, grief stopped being a stranger and instead became more of an uninvited guest that clearly planned to overstay its welcome. We learned to live with grief, to develop a new semblance of normalcy that involved its constant presence. Eventually the ranks of people praying for us had to thin out, the supports from church and neighbors had to dry up. Eventually we had to learn to live this new life God has called us to. And if in the early days we needed strength to keep our heads above water, strength to simply keep us from drowning in sorrow, we now need endurance, the fortitude to carry a heavy burden through a long journey.

Today Aileen is feeling ill, so Michaela has come to the cemetery with me instead. As we drive, we talk about her loss, about her sorrow, about her favorite memories of her only brother. I am struck again that even as we each carry our own sorrow, we also carry one another's. Even as I grieve my own loss, I also grieve hers, for deeper even than the sorrow of suffering a great bereavement is the sorrow of watching my wife and daughters endure one. It is grief added to grief, sorrow atop sorrow, burden upon burden.

We walk to the grave together and water the grass, a rectangle of healthy green that sharply contrasts with the burnt brown around it. Michaela remains behind while I refill the watering cans. And as I set out on the return journey, I realize how weary I am—weary with the physical burden of carrying cans of water, but even more so, with the spiritual and emotional burden of grief. It takes no great strength to carry a watering can for one minute or two, for three steps or four. But as the distance grows longer, the burden grows heavier and the body weaker. What was easy at the beginning can be excruciating by the end. A journey that began with great vigor can soon devolve into a long and difficult slog. And so it is with our grief.

Midway through my journey, my eye falls on a gravestone. Beneath the name of another young man and the dates that record the brief span of his life, it says only this: "Courage, dear heart." Immediately, I recognize the words. They come from the mind of Lucy Pevensie, the heart of Aslan, and the pen of

C. S. Lewis. In one of Lewis's Narnia books, a little ship called the *Dawn Treader* is far out to sea and in great peril. A darkness has set in and will not lift. The crew is in terror, uncertain if they will live to see a new day. Desperate, young Lucy whispers, "Aslan, Aslan, if ever you loved us at all, send us help now." Soon there is a little glimmer of light, then a growing and full beam like a spotlight, then a great albatross that swoops out of the heavens to lead them to safety. And as they are delivered from their great trial, "no one except Lucy knew that as it circled the mast it had whispered to her, 'Courage, dear heart.'" The voice, she felt sure, belonged to Aslan.[1]

I am aware of no great peril in these days and do not need the kind of courage that shored up the crew of the *Dawn Treader* as they faced the terror of darkness. I need courage of another kind. I recently remarked to Aileen that while I still associate Nick with my past and future, I no longer associate him with my present. I love him more than ever—absence does make the heart grow fonder. But I no longer expect to see his face or hear his voice. I no longer have that sense that I am locked in an awful dream and will soon wake up. My grief has advanced from a sharp pain to something more like a dull ache. And I know this is an ache I will carry for the rest of my days.

The courage I need now is the courage to face a lifetime of grief, the courage to bear up under a great bereavement, the courage to face a long sorrow with faithful perseverance. I need resolve, I need determination, I need whatever it takes to remain loyal to God and submitted to his purposes. I need strength to press on in the presence of pain, strength to endure all the way to the end of the journey he has marked out for me. And as I pause for just a moment to shift the watering cans in my hand, I hear the whisper too, a whisper that gives the very thing it speaks. "Courage, dear heart," it says. And the voice, I feel sure, belongs to Jesus.

CHAPTER 33

the ministry of sorrow

Death is the great interrupter. Death is the great interrupter because, far more often than not, it strikes when it's least expected. When death comes—and especially when it comes to the young—it interrupts plans, dreams, projects, and goals. One author observes how very sad, how very pathetic it is, when a man dies suddenly and we go into his home or place of business "and see the unfinished things he has left—a letter half written, a book half read, a picture begun but not completed. Life is full of mere fragments," he observes, "mere beginnings of things."[1]

I went into Nick's dorm room a couple of days after his death to sort through his personal effects, to determine what should be kept and what should be given away. His room gave every indication that he had expected to return. Books lay waiting on his desk in preparation for final essays. Hebrew was jotted all over his whiteboard in preparation for exams. Spreadsheets full of guest lists were open on his computer in preparation for his wedding. I'm sure he was as surprised as we were that all of these tasks would be left forever incomplete, that they would only ever be mere fragments, mere beginnings of things.

And it wasn't just *his* life that was so suddenly and significantly interrupted. The day before he died I, too, was full of plans. I had just begun my next big book project. I had just jotted the opening sentences of the book I intended to write after that. I was deep into various threads of research and was learning to master new software designed to organize and express ideas. My mind was full of beginnings of things. But the day after Nick's death, those things, too, had been set aside and very nearly forgotten. What seemed so urgent and so important the day before seemed nearly irrelevant the day after.

I eventually picked up some of those threads and brought to completion some of those beginnings, but only a few. Nick's death has given me a revised sense of what is important, of what merits my attention, of what is worth pursuing. Not only that, but God has used it to redirect my way. If death is the great interrupter, it has also been the great redirector. Nick's death was not the end of my calling in life but a new beginning to it. It hasn't closed out my story, but it has opened a new chapter for me. If each of us is called by God to take up some kind of ministry, Nick's death has called and equipped me to take up a new kind, a ministry I wasn't expecting.

An old legend tells of the construction of one of England's great cathedrals and of the master builder, who, having carefully drawn up his plans, traveled to a nearby quarry to choose the stones that would make up his masterpiece. He cast his discerning eye on the great collection gathered for his inspection and began to picture in his mind which would be appropriate to each purpose—which were suited for the firm foundations and strong pillars, which were just right for the mighty buttresses and towering spires. With confidence he selected one particularly rough-hewn stone, then took his hammer in one hand and chisel in the other. As the builder began to rain blows on the stone, it cried out in pain, but the builder comforted it by explaining that it must be shaped to take its place in his great work of art. If only it could endure the pain, it would see that his plan was good. And sure enough, when the master builder was finished, the stone was carefully fitted into the chancel, where it bore witness through the centuries to the genius of the builder.[2]

Just so, our God knows how to fit each of his people into his church, for like the builder of legend, he is creating a masterpiece that will showcase his genius and cause all who see it to glorify his name. And just as the builder fits the stone to the purpose, God fits the people to the plan. God equips his people in different ways, gifts them with different passions, and calls them to different ministries—some to exhortation and some to evangelism, some to leading and some to teaching, some to acts of generosity and some to acts of mercy.

And God calls some to a ministry of sorrow. For just as he calls some to proclaim his gospel in far-off lands, he calls some to bear witness to his goodness in grief. Just as he calls some to bravely face the fire of persecution, he calls some to courageously face the pain of bereavement. Just as he calls some to give generously and some to act mercifully, he calls some to grieve faithfully. And I'm convinced this is a ministry God has called me to—the ministry of sorrow, a ministry of faithful suffering.

I could only be fitted to this ministry by a great loss. The one called to preach must have the ability to communicate; the one called to sing must have musical talent; the one called to generosity must have something to give. And the one called to the ministry of sorrow must suffer loss. If the laying on of hands ordained me for my ministry of pastoring, the tearing of Nick out of my hands ordained me for this ministry of sorrow. Nick's death is the hammer and chisel of the builder, and I, like the stone, have cried out under the pain of it. But Nick's death is also the qualification that has equipped me to take up the ministry God has called me to. If the stone must trust the builder to fit the stone to the building, I must trust God to fit the man to the temple—the living temple he is constructing in which the apostles are the foundation, in which Christ himself is the cornerstone, and where each of us finds our place and purpose as bricks in the wall.[3]

It was no small thing I was doing when I came to Christ, no small thing to bow the knee to Jesus and consecrate myself to his purposes. It was no small thing to sing, "All to Jesus I surrender, all to Him I freely give,"[4] or, "Take my life and let it be consecrated, Lord, to thee."[5] It was no small thing to pray, "Thy kingdom come. Thy will be done," or, "Not my will, but thine, be done." It was no small thing, for I knew that God would take me at my word. When God called me to come to him, he called every part of me to come—and to come all the way. To him I surrendered my time, my money, my gifts, my dreams, my desires. To him I surrendered my very life. And to him I surrendered the one thing I count dearer than life—my family.

When I came to Christ, I offered myself to him to be used for his purposes rather than mine, to pursue his glory rather than my own. It has often been my prayer that God would make me useful, that he would equip me to minister in the way that is most needful. So how could I now rebel? How could I now complain? He has done no more than I have invited him to do.

Why would God call me to the ministry of sorrow? I don't know. He hasn't told me and doesn't owe me an explanation. But I am convinced that he expects me to let sorrow do its work in me. I must not be enslaved to it or made useless by it. He doesn't want me to waste the rest of my life incapacitated by that sorrow, but rather to allow it to motivate me to glorify him by doing good to others.

Through this ministry of sorrow, I can testify before a skeptical world that one who praises God in the giving can also praise him in the taking, that one who honors God in times of great joy will still honor him in times of great loss. I can bear witness that faith can survive sorrow, that we can be content even in loss, that when we are weak, then we are truly strong, for it is when we are weak that he provides us with his strength.

And through this ministry, I can come alongside others who face a similar loss and minister to them in their sorrow, comfort them with the comfort with which I myself have been comforted by God.[6] I have been equipped now to bear their burdens and so fulfill the law of Christ.[7] I have been given what I need to truly weep with those who weep, for they will be crying the very same tears that have so often filled my own eyes.[8] In these ways, and others besides, I can carry out this new ministry God has called me to.

I'm not the same man I was when Nick was alive. I'm deeply wounded, deeply scarred, deeply broken. Yet I know it is God who decreed this suffering, and I accept it as something meaningful, something precious, something sacred. I accept it as training for a ministry he has called me to. I'm ready to learn and to apply its lessons, painful though they may be. I know I'll be made better by it, made kinder, gentler, more empathetic, more sanctified, and more useful. I know that God has not called me away from duty but toward a new duty. He has not interrupted my usefulness to him but has redirected it. And where he leads, I must follow. Where he leads, I *will* follow.

god, give me sons

I loved being father to a son. I loved being father to the kind of son Solomon commended when he said, "A wise son brings joy to his father."[1] Truly, Nick was a son who made his father proud—so very proud to call him my own. He was, in so many ways, the joy of my heart.

I miss being father to a son. I so dreadfully miss the simple pleasure of hearing a masculine voice say, "Dad." I miss having someone following closely in my footsteps, someone who is observing me, imitating me, expecting me to lead the way he will follow. I miss knowing there is someone who is looking to me to set a worthy example of a husband, father, pastor, Christian. For two decades, this was one of my most sacred and most precious callings. And then, in an instant, it wasn't. The father instinct that was so strong within me went from abundant to empty. And so while I miss Nick so very deeply, I also miss the part of my life and identity that was wrapped up in being his dad, in being father to a son. His death has left more than one kind of void.

I'm sure this is no new insight into grief, but it is one I have learned only by experience—that some losses are not only losses of a person but also of an identity. We don't only grieve the person who is gone, but also the part of our identity that departed with them. It has taken me some time to understand this, to process it, to acknowledge it. Yet as I look back, I can see it dawning in a quiet and subconscious way.

In the very early days that followed that tragic night, I found a prayer arising spontaneously within my heart: "God, give me sons." This is a prayer that has been on my lips often in the past year. It is not a petition I arrived at thoughtfully or deliberately, but one that simply welled up from inside, one that perhaps sought to fill a gaping hole, to soothe an agonizing wound, to satisfy a deep longing.

I confess that I don't even really know what my prayer means or how I expect God to answer it. Though I serve the same God as did Abraham and Zechariah, I don't anticipate that God will answer this prayer by giving me biological sons. And though I have two daughters whom I trust will introduce sons-in-law into our family,[2] and though I very much look forward to being a kind of dad to them, I sense there may be more to the matter than this. But exactly what, I don't know. I don't have any clarity, any insight, any guesses. Only prayers.

Of course God does not satisfy every longing on this side of eternity and does not answer every prayer with a clear and unambiguous yes. He owes me no answer, and I have no right to demand one. Yet if God does love me as a father loves a son, wouldn't this be the kind of prayer he would be likely to answer?

Wouldn't this be the kind of prayer he himself might put on my heart?

I don't know what the years will bring. I don't know how many the Lord has assigned to me. I have never been more aware of my dependence on his providence and never been more willing to acknowledge that God is ordering this world according to his inscrutable wisdom. I have never been more willing to simply trust him with my life, my heart, my prayers. And so, for the time being, I will continue to pray with hope, with faith, and even with some expectation. I'll continue to pray, "God, give me sons." And I'll anticipate how God may respond, how God may direct, how God may answer the longing of my aching heart.

CHAPTER 35

in green pastures

No work of art is more beautiful, more valuable, more irre-
placeable, than the Twenty-third Psalm. It has stood through
the ages as a work of art more exquisite than *The Night Watch*,
more faultless than *Mona Lisa*, more thought-provoking than
Starry Night. The lines of the greatest poets cannot match its
imagery, the words of the greatest theologians its profundity.
Credentialed academics may wrestle with it, yet young children
can understand it. It is read over cradles and cribs, over coffins
and crypts, at births and deaths, at weddings and funerals. It is
prayed in closets, sung in churches, and chanted in cathedrals.

This psalm dries more crying eyes, raises more drooping
hands, and strengthens more weakened knees than any man
or angel. It tends to every kind of wound and ministers to
every kind of sorrow. To trade it for all the wealth of all the
worlds would be the worst of bargains. I'd have rather penned
the Twenty-third Psalm than written *Hamlet*, than painted
Sunflowers, than sculpted *The Thinker*, for when Shakespeare's
play has been forgotten, when van Gogh's painting has faded,

when Rodin's sculpture has been destroyed, David's song will remain. We impoverish ourselves if we do not read it, do not meditate upon it, and do not treasure it. We weaken ourselves if we do not drink deeply of it in our deepest sorrows.

David's great psalm employs the simplest of images—that of a shepherd and his sheep—and assures of the greatest of truths: God is forever present with his people. "The LORD is my shepherd," he says so simply. "I shall not want."[1] Because the Lord is his shepherd, this sheep can have confidence that he will never lack for any necessity, for the shepherd loves his flock and will faithfully attend to their every need. When they are tired, he will make them lie down in green pastures; when they are thirsty, he will lead them beside still waters; when they are downtrodden, he will restore them; when they are lost or uncertain, he will lead them in the right paths. The sheep can rest in peace under the shepherd's watchful eye. They can be assured of every comfort under his tender care.

But sometimes fields go barren and springs run dry. And in such times, the good shepherd knows just what to do; he knows he must lead his sheep to fresh pastures and to cool, still waters. Yet he also knows that the way will be difficult, for these pastures and waters lie on the far side of a dark valley. So he calls his sheep to himself and begins to lead them into the darkness, to lead them along an unfamiliar path.

And here, on the edge of uncertainty, sheep says to shepherd, "Even though I walk through the valley of the shadow of death, I will fear no evil, for you are with me."[2] Though the shepherd must lead his sheep into the darkness, lead them through unknown valleys, they will go, for he is with them. Their fears are soothed by his strength, their uncertainty by his presence. When enemies approach, he will ward them off with his rod; when sheep stumble; he will lift them with his staff.

And soon enough, sheep and shepherd will emerge into the light on the far side of their darkness. And there again they will settle together for rest and refreshment. There again they will dwell in sweet peace.

The shepherd who leads them in will lead them through and lead them out.

What comfort there is in the knowledge that the shepherd who tends his sheep alongside still waters is the very same shepherd who tends them in the valley of darkness. The sheep do not foolishly blunder into that valley. They are not led there by wily wolves or chased there by hungry bears. They are led there by their loving shepherd; they enter there only according to his good plan and perfect purpose. They enter the valley only because it is for their benefit, only because the shepherd is leading them to something better beyond. They are never for a moment alone, for they are always following him.

My shepherd has called me to walk a difficult path—a path of sorrow, a path of grief, a path stained by tears. The way is uncharted to me but familiar to him, for he sees the end from the beginning; he has known from ancient times the things still undone. He speaks to the darkness and declares, "My counsel shall stand, and I will accomplish all my purpose."[3] I can have in him all the confidence of a sheep in his shepherd. I can follow him, knowing that "surely goodness and mercy shall follow me all the days of my life, and I shall dwell in the house of the LORD forever."[4]

And I *will* follow him, singing this song in the darkness, meditating upon its truths with every step. I'd rather face my trial with David's psalm in my heart than with Aaron's staff in my hand, with Joshua's army at my side, with Solomon's gold in my pocket. I'd rather know the words to this one song than of all the great hymns of the Christian faith. I'd rather lose everything with my shepherd beside me than gain the whole world alone. Yes, I can bear the loss of my son as long as I know the presence of my shepherd. I can walk this path, I can pass through this dark valley, if only my shepherd guides me, if only he leads the way.[5]

my most precious possession

I once heard of an old man who, for as long as anyone could remember, had carried a little wooden box wherever he went. When he visited customers and clients, the box traveled with him. When he worshiped at church, the box was at his side. When he slept in his bed, the box was on his nightstand. He even made careful provision for it in his final will and testament. Legends grew up to guess what was in the box. Some said money, some jewelry, others diamonds. But when the day came and he finally passed away, they were all proven wrong. The box was opened, and those who were there saw that it contained nothing more than a few little playthings that had belonged to his darling child who had died many years before. These were the man's most precious possessions, his most sacred treasures.

And they *were* treasures, because while they may have had no value in the eyes of others, they had immeasurable value in his, since they had belonged to one he had loved and lost, one who had been taken from his arms and delivered to the angels'. They were reminders of bright moments and happy days, and tokens of even better moments and even more blessed days ahead. As he gazed at them, as he touched them, as he pondered them, they carried his mind backward and forward, to the past and the future, to days on earth and days in heaven. In some way, these objects spanned the vast distance between the man and his child, between the living and the dead.[1]

Though I cannot hold against Nick something that is actually a virtue, I almost wish he had cared more for possessions. I almost wish he had left behind a few treasured objects, a few items that he loved and valued above all others. Had he done so, I might have been tempted to build a box and carry it with me at all times. But as it is, he cared little for stuff. If he had food to eat, clothing to wear, a book to read, and a computer to work on, he was content.

He did, however, leave behind a Bible. When he resolved that he wanted to pursue ministry and when he proved it by enrolling in seminary, his mother and I presented him with a Bible—the kind that would suit a pastor and endure through a long career of preaching, teaching, and counseling. On the inscription page, I wrote some simple words to encourage him to live and to minister according to the Word of God.

As far as I know, he preached from that Bible only once. During a summer internship at our church, he was given the opportunity to lead an evening service. He opened his Bible and taught just a small portion of it—a miniature message based on infallible truth. I could not have been more proud—proud to see him teaching and, even more so, proud to see his commitment to the Word of God, in this, his only sermon.

That Bible was one of the few items we set aside when we cleaned out his dorm room, one of the few of his belongings we brought back home with us. For a time it sat on a shelf, until I had the idea of asking my father-in-law to make a display cabinet for it. He got to work and built a beautiful teak stand and glass case—a fitting home for a precious possession.

A few years ago, I traveled the world to search for historical objects through which I could tell the story of the Christian faith. I found hundreds of noteworthy candidates, many of which were Bibles. In a little basement office in Oxford, I took William Carey's Bible from a case that had been built from his old shoemaker's bench. In an archive in Belfast, I read the margin notes from Amy Carmichael's Bible, and in a one-room museum in Bristol, I read James 1:27 from George Müller's. In a seminary in Sydney, I leafed through a first-edition King James that is worth as much as a house, and in Manchester, I gazed at a papyrus fragment of the book of John that is worth many times more. Each of these Bibles was a wonder, each of them a part of history.[2] But I would not trade a single one for the simple black leather-bound English Standard Version Bible that rests in the case near my desk.

As that old man would from time to time open his little wooden box and gaze on the playthings that had once been held in the hands of his child, I often gaze at that Bible and let it remind me of Nick, for in its own way, it spans the distance between father and son, between the one left and the one gone on ahead. And though the object itself can do little to console me, the words it displays can do much more, for I have laid it open to 1 Corinthians 15, with its words of grace, hope, mystery, and victory. These words, read so powerfully at Nick's memorial service, remind me of truth when my memory fades, shore up my faith when my heart grows weary. They remind me that Christ's triumph over death was also mine—and also Nick's. They remind me that death itself has been vanquished in the death of Christ, so that "as in Adam all die, so also in Christ shall all be made alive."[3]

And on days when a particularly deep sorrow washes over me, on days when it seems as if I may be overwhelmed, I raise the glass and take the Bible from its case. I rest it in my lap, leaf through its pages, and imagine my precious boy doing the same. I read some of its promises and smile to think that Nick has already seen the best of them fulfilled. Then, placing the Bible back in its case, I thank God for the young man who once owned it, the young man who once held it, the young man who once received it from my hand and then gave it back.

CHAPTER 37

nothing he needs

"What is your servant, that you should notice a dead dog like me?" These disbelieving words come from the mouth of Mephibosheth when he is told he will now and from this moment forward be welcome to dine at the table of the king and have restored to him the estates of his fathers. In a moment he is plucked from obscurity and delivered to honor, for in a moment the king has stopped treating him like a subject and begun treating him like a son.[1]

The Bible provides many examples of love between friends, but none is more instructive than that of David for Jonathan. The kindness David shows to lowly Mephibosheth is not first directed toward him, but toward his father, for the son comes to David's attention only after the king asks his servants, "Is there still anyone left of the house of Saul, that I may show him kindness for Jonathan's sake?"[2]

David has long since suffered the grievous loss of his closest friend, but he has never lost his love for him. Though the souls that were knit together in life have been torn apart by death, the affection remains strong. Though David can no longer speak with his friend, no longer enjoy his fellowship, no longer encourage him or be encouraged by him, his heart is still warm toward him. Now, since he can no longer express that love directly, he chooses to express it indirectly, creatively, generously. The one thing David can do to love Jonathan is to love the son of Jonathan.

As Christians we are accustomed to hearing that love is a verb, that love is not meant to be merely felt but to be done. We do our children no good if we have warm feelings for them but refuse to feed or clothe them. We do the world no good if we feel great sympathy for the state of lost souls but neglect to tell anyone about Jesus. Religion that is pure and undefiled before the Father is not the religion that feels much, but the religion that does much—that visits orphans in their affliction and ministers to widows in their grief.[3] Feelings are meant to provoke action so that hearts of love direct deeds of love. That being the case, one of the great sorrows that comes with the death of a loved one is being left with feelings that can no longer be acted on.

For twenty years I loved to love Nick. I loved to feel love for him but, even better, to do love for him, to set my affections into action, for fatherhood is all about loving, about giving, about caring. Caring for him and for his sisters has been one of my greatest joys, serving them one of my highest honors, spoiling them one of my dearest pleasures. For years I counted it joy to make their school lunches, to package up sandwiches and cookies and juice boxes, each combination personalized just a little bit according to their preferences. I loved creating the tradition of inviting one of them to the local diner for breakfast each Saturday, so we could simply enjoy one another as we chatted over bacon, eggs, and toast. As they've grown older and begun to get jobs, I've established the habit of making sure I'm up before they are so I can brew their morning coffee and hug them as they head out the door. No one should have to face a hard day's work without a hug. And then there's the tremendous privilege of prayer. I always wanted them to know that before their day began, I had already prayed for them. What an honor, what a blessing it has been to intercede for them day by day.

I have been looking forward to the next stage of loving my children—a stage in which I will be loving them as adults, as peers, as husbands and wives. I have been looking forward to loving my children's children. As always, Nick would be the trailblazer. To prepare myself I spoke with friends who have children older than mine. I asked their counsel on how best to love older children, how to serve and surprise them in adulthood as I have so loved to do in childhood. They were full of wise counsel about loving them, affirming them, spoiling them. I was excited to begin putting their wisdom into action.

But then there was nothing more I could do, no more actions I could take on Nick's behalf. All the feelings of love remain and are even greater through the lens of loss. But the ability to love him is as far gone as he is. Where before I could always speak a kind word to him or send him a small gift, now he is beyond the benefit of my encouragement. He can no longer receive the tokens of my affection. My love is strong, but my mouth has been rendered silent, my hands powerless. There is nothing he needs, nothing I can get for him, nothing I can offer him, nothing I can do for him, nothing I can even pray for him. The best I've been able to come up with is taking cups of coffee to the cemetery, pulling weeds from the grass that lies atop his grave, tending a miniature garden up against his monument. But I know these pathetic little gestures are for me and not for him. I hate this inability. I hate this emptiness. I hate this impotence.

I find myself wondering if this sense of helplessness is why Roman Catholics are drawn to the doctrine of purgatory. Catholic doctrine states that the souls of Christians are not immediately ushered into heaven but must first enter a place of purgation, where through suffering, they are purified of whatever sin remains. It becomes the responsibility of loved ones to intercede on their behalf, to pray for them, to initiate Masses for them, to do what they can to shorten that terrible time of suffering. Of course, I'm convinced the gospel of justification by grace alone through faith alone negates the very notion of purgatory, so I am confident it does not exist. Still, I understand something of its appeal. There is nothing I wouldn't buy, nothing I wouldn't acquire, nothing I wouldn't do, nothing I wouldn't initiate, if only it would serve Nick, if only it would let me express my love.

But the reality is that there is nothing Nick needs. This feels like a hard truth, but I know it is actually a very good one. There is nothing Nick needs, because he is in that place where all his needs have been met. There is nothing he lacks, because he is in the place where he lacks no good thing. There is nothing I can do for him, because Jesus has done all that is necessary;

nothing I can give, because Jesus gave his own life's blood; nothing I can pay, because Jesus paid it all. If Nick has any unmet desire, any unfulfilled longing, it is only this: that history would come to its great consummation in the return of Jesus Christ. He, with the saints and martyrs, must even now be crying out, "How long, O Lord? How long?"[4]

Yet David teaches me that even though there is nothing Nick needs, this does not mean I am powerless in expressing my love. Like David, I can ask, "Is there still anyone left who was loved by Nick, that I may show them kindness for Nick's sake?" I can express my love by caring for the people he cared for—his mother, his sisters, his fiancée. I loved these people before, of course, but am committed to loving them all the more, that I may honor my son, my brother and friend. My love for them can be a tribute to him, an expression of my loyalty. And as I express my love for him through my love for them, I'll be anticipating the day when the great chasm between us has finally been bridged, when I once again see him face-to-face, when I can once again show him the love that even now brings warmth to my heart, a tremble to my lips, and a tear to my eye.

i miss my son today

I miss my son today. That goes without saying, I suppose, since I miss him every day. But on this day, the pain is particularly sharp, the ache especially deep. I miss my friend and brother; I miss my protégé. I miss the son of my youth, the delight of my heart. I miss seeing him and hugging him. I miss teaching him and learning from him. I miss the sound of his voice and the cackle of his laugh. I miss having a son at all. I just plain miss my Nick.

The time between now and when he went to heaven has passed so quickly, yet so slowly. It often feels like it was just yesterday that we received the phone call, just yesterday that we endured the funeral, just yesterday that we watched the casket being lowered into the cold, dark ground. But at the same time, it feels like it was a lifetime ago. We were different people back then, a different family with different desires, different assumptions, a different understanding of life and death and the God who is sovereign over it all.

And just as the time between now and when Nick went to heaven has passed both quickly and slowly, I expect that the time between now and when I go to heaven will pass both quickly and slowly. This life is a dash, a blip, a vapor, yet just as truly a slog, a marathon, a long and wearying pilgrimage. I have begun to notice that while the brevity of life is best seen in retrospect, it's the slowness of life that tends to be felt in the moment. It may be brief as we look back on it, but it's long as we live it.

And it feels long today. It looks long today. It looks long as I gaze into the future and see a road laid out before me that may well lead through months, years, and decades. It looks longer still as I consider the heavy burden of grief God has called me to carry. I am confident I can carry a great weight for a short distance but far less confident that I can carry it for many miles or many years. I just don't know how I will bear up under this sorrow if I have to carry it all the way to the end.

My father was a landscaper, and he used to take me to work with him from time to time. I remember one day when he brought me with him to be an unskilled but low-cost source of manual labor. He showed me a skid of bricks that had been delivered to the end of a client's driveway and then a walkway he was building to the front door. My job was to get the bricks from the first spot to the second. I remember gazing at that giant pile with despair. How could I, at twelve or thirteen years of age, possibly move what looked like a literal ton of bricks? I realized I would have to do it in the only way I could. Piece by piece, brick by brick, step by step, I carried each one to my father. He laid them as quickly as I could bring them to him until a perfect path led to the entrance of that beautiful home.

And just so, while God has called me to bear my grief for

a lifetime, and to do so faithfully, he has not called me to bear the entire weight of it all at once. As the pile is made up of many bricks, a lifetime is made up of many days. The burden of a whole lifetime's grief would be far too heavy to bear, and the challenge of a whole lifetime's faithfulness far too daunting to consider. But the God who knows my frailty has broken down that assignment into little parts, little days, and has promised a grace that is sufficient for each one of them. My challenge for today is not to bear the grief of a lifetime or to be faithful to the end, but only to carry today's grief and only to be faithful on this one little day that he has spread out before me.

And I am confident that by his grace I can carry out today's assignment. I am confident that I can bear the burden of this day's sorrow until night falls and my eyes close in rest. I am confident that I can be faithful in today's calling for as long as the day lasts. I don't need to think about tomorrow or next week or next year. I don't need the strength to carry the burdens of any other day or the resolve to remain faithful through any other circumstance. My God-given task began this morning and extends only until tonight. Then, when I awake again tomorrow with the dawning of a new day, I will awaken to new blessings, new strength, and new grace that will allow me to be strong and faithful through that day as well.

And in just that way—brick by brick, step by step, day by day—he will lead me, he will keep me, he will enable me to be strong and faithful in all that he calls me to. And as I serve my Father in the assignment he has given me, I know that each brick, each step, each day, is bringing me a little bit closer to the entrance of that great home he is preparing for me.

CHAPTER 39

death did him
no harm

One of the great and enduring poems of the English language—
one I memorized as a child and have recited countless times
since—was written specifically to ridicule death. Displaying a
profound mastery of language, meter, and rhyme, John Donne
mocks and belittles death for falsely convincing so many of its
power, so many of its strength, so many of its horrors. In "Holy
Sonnet X," better known as "Death, Be Not Proud," Donne
personifies Death so he can pull back the curtain and expose
the fraud skulking behind:

> Death, be not proud, though some have called thee
> Mighty and dreadful, for thou art not so.[1]

Many of us regard Death as mighty and dreadful and
worthy of our greatest fear. Many of us live our entire lives with
trepidation as we await its inevitable approach. Some barely live,

or live half-heartedly, for fear of Death. Little wonder, then, that Death has become haughty, proud, and conceited, convinced of its own power and might.

But the reality is very different. As the poet continues, he offers a whole catalog of ways in which Death fails to carry out its threats, ways in which Death has been rendered ultimately harmless toward those who are loved by God. Death, he points out, does not actually kill us but only delivers us to rest and sleep. Death does not truly rob us of life but only separates our souls from our bodies for a time. Death takes no initiative but is only ever a slave to the actions of others. And then, even as Death threatens each one of us, it lives in constant fear, always aware that the greatest of all deaths will be its own. For as Donne says in his powerful concluding couplet:

> One short sleep past, we wake eternally
> And death shall be no more; Death, thou shalt die.

Indeed, the Bible describes Death as the final enemy, and though it will be last to fall, its time will certainly come.[2] The death of Death has already been guaranteed by the crucifixion and resurrection of Jesus Christ. Its final day and hour have already been fixed in the mind of God, and it now simply awaits the moment of his choosing. As one little word shall fully and finally end the reign of Satan, so too the reign of Death. Death, we learn, is a defeated adversary, a flaccid foe, a chained enemy who can go not one step farther than God allows.

Now, with the mind of the poet I look to Death and goad him as well.[3]

Death, did you bring any great harm to Nick when you released his spirit from his body? Surely not, for all you did was deliver him from physical pain and deliver him to spiritual blessings. You liberated him from all strife and strain, from all sorrow and suffering, from all anxiety and uncertainty. You delivered him to the fullest peace and the sweetest comfort. Death, be not proud!

Death, did you bring any great harm to Nick when you took him from my side? No, for when you took Nick from my side, you delivered him to the Savior's. You transported him to that place where he can receive his welcome and his reward, where he can see his Savior's face, where he can express his deepest gratitude to the One who healed him and made him whole. Death, be not proud!

Death, did you bring any great harm to Nick when you carried him away from this place of toil, away from this place that so constantly strains body, mind, and spirit? No, for he has now been given rest—rest from all that aggrieves, rest from all that perplexes, rest from all that discourages. He no longer has to strive against sin or labor toward holiness; he no longer faces trials and no longer endures temptations; he no longer sins and is no longer sinned against. He is now fully equipped to perfectly serve the Savior he loves so well. Death, be not proud!

Death, did you bring any great harm to Nick when you called him away from his earthly home? No, for you merely called Nick away from this foreign land in which he was only ever a sojourner and took him to that new land where he had long since secured full citizenship. You transported him from this place of faith to that place of sight, from this shadow to that light, from this foretaste to that reality, from an earthly tent to a celestial palace. Death, be not proud!

Death, did you bring any great harm to Nick when you pulled him away from his family? By no means, for you simply delivered him to the community above, to the great company of saints that stands in the presence of Christ to worship him perfectly and unendingly. There he has joined with the saints and martyrs, the elders and angels, to pour out his perfect praise and perfect prayers to his perfect God. Death, be not proud!

Death, though you may think you are a master, you are but a servant. Though you may think you are mighty, you have only the limited shreds of power that God has granted you. Though you may think you are scary, I laugh in your face. You may be convinced that because you have walked this earth since the days of the garden, you will walk it forever, but listen, and you will hear that the clock is ticking; look, and you will see that the sands of time are sinking; think, and you will know that your doom is fast approaching. For to the same degree that the death and resurrection of Jesus Christ guaranteed the lives of those he loves, it guaranteed your demise.

And on that day, not one will mourn, not one will weep, not one will shed a single tear for you. To the contrary, we will sing, we will celebrate, we will party and rejoice, we will dance upon your grave. Death, raise your chin and look me in the eye as I say it: You did Jesus no harm, you can do me no harm, and you did my Nick no harm. Death, be not proud, for one short sleep past, *we* wake eternally, and *you* shall be no more. Death, *you* shall die!

> Death, be not proud, though some have called thee
> Mighty and dreadful, for thou art not so;
> For those whom thou think'st thou dost overthrow
> Die not, poor Death, nor yet canst thou kill me.
> From rest and sleep, which but thy pictures be,
> Much pleasure; then from thee much more must flow,
> And soonest our best men with thee do go,
> Rest of their bones, and soul's delivery.
> Thou art slave to fate, chance, kings, and desperate men,
> And dost with poison, war, and sickness dwell,
> And poppy or charms can make us sleep as well
> And better than thy stroke; why swell'st thou then?
> One short sleep past, we wake eternally
> And death shall be no more; Death, thou shalt die.

CHAPTER 40

it's time to rise!

I awake early, too rested to remain in bed but too tired to function. I stumble down the stairs, press the "start" button on the coffee maker, then collapse on the couch as I wait for it to brew. In those few moments, I drift back to sleep and have the most vivid of dreams.

In my dream, I see myself lying back in bed when an angelic envoy rouses me with a message. And as surely as Mary knew, as surely as Joseph knew, as surely as Zechariah knew, in my dream I know—I know the messenger is reliable and his message authentic. "God sent me to tell you that Christ will return in exactly one hour." My heart rises. My mind reels. My feet race. Leaping from bed, I run downstairs, grab my coat and keys, and sprint out the door. I know exactly where I need to be.

One scene fades into the next, and I see myself arriving at Glen Oaks Cemetery. Flinging the car door open, I leap into the predawn darkness. Up and down the rows of graves I begin to run, shouting out the glad tidings. "It's time! It's time!" I cry out. "It's time to rise!" I run up one row and down the next, up one row and down the next, my feet pounding over the uneven turf.

I watch myself pause briefly by the grave of the young man whose parents have chosen to inscribe it with just three brief words—the words Aslan whispered to Lucy when she was overwhelmed with fear and uncertainty: "Courage, dear heart."[1] And though those words have so often blessed and strengthened me, this morning I have no need of encouragement. "Caleb," I cry out, "it's time! It's time to rise. Just a few more minutes, and it's time!"

I take off running once more but pause almost immediately, this time by a nearby grave where, just a few short weeks ago, a family gathered to sing sweet hymns of comfort in both English and Hindi. "It's time, my Christian sister," I say in a shout. "It's time to rise!"

I see myself running on and on, up and down the silent rows, crying out the news. I stop again, this time by a plot where another young man is buried, a young man whose parents once approached Aileen and me to encourage us, to console us, to pray down heaven's comfort upon us. "It's time!" I shout. "It's time. Just a few more moments and you will rise! Your body and soul will be joined together and you'll rise! It's time!"

The eastern horizon is beginning to glow with the first light of day. The earliest rays of the sun are threatening to break through the clouds hanging low over Lake Ontario. The clock has ticked down to just one minute, and now my feet carry me to the spot in that cemetery that has become most familiar.

With my face glowing golden with the sunrise, I pause

where I've paused so often. On the edge of that patch of grass that has been tended by my hand and watered by my tears, I drop to my knees. In a tone that is confident and unwavering, I say, "It's time, my boy! It's time! Just one more minute and we'll hear the cry of command. Just one more moment and we'll hear the voice of the archangel. Just a few more seconds and we'll hear the blast of the trumpet. It's time, my boy. It's time. It's time to wake up. It's time to rise!" I begin the final countdown: 5 . . . 4 . . . 3 . . . 2 . . . 1 . . .

And then—and then I become aware again. I become aware that I am on my couch, not in the cemetery. I become aware that it has been a dream, not reality. But I also become aware that my face is wet with tears and my heart rich with joy. For though it has only been a dream, it is a dream that somehow has meditated on the best of all promises, the surest of all hopes. It is a dream that in some shape and some form will most certainly come true, for God has given us his unfailing word:

> For the Lord himself will descend from heaven with a cry of command, with the voice of an archangel, and with the sound of the trumpet of God. And the dead in Christ will rise first. Then we who are alive, who are left, will be caught up together with them in the clouds to meet the Lord in the air, and so we will always be with the Lord.[2]

footprints on the sands of time

I once spent a meditative morning exploring one of London's ancient burial grounds. Walking solemnly past the endless graves in Bunhill Fields, I realized I was among my people, surrounded by kindred spirits, for on the tombs and the headstones I saw many names of individuals who have influenced my life and shaped my faith. The great John Bunyan lies beneath a stately monument, as does John Owen. Nearby are Joseph Hart, Isaac Watts, and Susanna Wesley. Thomas Goodwin is there too, along with Nathaniel Vincent and John Gill. It is a great company of great saints, lying close together as they await the day of resurrection.

Longfellow says, poetically:

> Lives of great men all remind us
> We can make our lives sublime,

And, departing, leave behind us
Footprints on the sands of time.[1]

Each of these people, in their own way, left their mark on the world and on me. Bunyan's *The Pilgrim's Progress* has provided whole generations with ways to understand the Christian's experience of this world. More than three centuries after Owen's death, *Overcoming Sin and Temptation* remains the pre-eminent treatment of the topic. The words of Hart and Watts still resound in churches every time we sing, "Come, ye sinners, poor and needy,"[2] or, "Joy to the world, the Lord is come!"[3] I've heard it said that Susanna Wesley's hand rings all the Methodist church bells around the globe, for she gave birth to the brothers who cofounded that great movement. The legacies of Goodwin, Vincent, and Gill live on through their works of theology. Each of these saints has left indelible footprints on the sands of time.

Longfellow believes, rightly, that such great lives are not meant merely to be memorialized, but imitated. They are not meant simply to inspire us, but to motivate us to create our own legacies of faithfulness:

Let us, then, be up and doing,
With a heart for any fate;
Still achieving, still pursuing,
Learn to labor and to wait.[4]

Well and good. But what of those who had little chance to be up and doing? What of those who lived short lives rather than long ones, who were taken in the time of preparation rather than of action, who went to the grave before they were able to make a name for themselves, to accumulate any great accomplishments? Do they leave any footprints on the sands of time? Or is it as if they never lived at all?

Nick had no great desire to make a name for himself. He had no interest in fame or notoriety. He was content to be unseen—in fact, he preferred it. But it still seems cruel that he would be forgotten altogether. Yet, honestly, what is there to remember him by? He leaves behind no theological tomes, no great works of art, no extraordinary achievements. He leaves behind no financial legacy to fund further kingdom expansion, no children to carry his genes to future generations. He was the last male in the Challies line, so even his surname will in the course of time disappear and be gone. It is almost as if his feet never passed through this world, as if he left no footprints at all.

I can't help but turn my mind back to Bunhill Fields and the true lesson of that hallowed place. The true lesson of that burial ground is not that most people leave indelible footprints on the sands of time, but that most do not, for while there are two thousand monuments in that cemetery, there are 120,000 bodies. While there are a few luminaries, there are far more "ordinaries." And who is to say their lives weren't every bit as sublime, every bit as noble, every bit as honoring to God? Do we really think that the only great lives are the lives that are remembered for being great?

Longfellow's poem has inspired many to be "up and doing," to give their lives to great attempts and great achievements.

But it has also inspired others to reflect realistically on the nature of life and death. I can't help but wonder if Hannah Flagg Gould had also walked through Bunhill Fields, if she had pondered, as I did, the vast quantities of nameless people lying beneath her feet. Perhaps they were on her mind when she began to write this poem:

> Alone I walked the ocean strand;
> A pearly shell was in my hand:
> I stooped, and wrote upon the sand
> My name—the year—the day.
> As onward from the spot I passed,
> One lingering look behind I cast:
> A wave came rolling high and fast,
> And washed my lines away.
>
> And so, methought, 't will shortly be
> With every mark on earth from me;
> A wave of dark oblivion's sea
> Will sweep across the place,
> Where I have trod the sandy shore
> Of time, and been, to be no more,
> Of me—my day—the name I bore,
> To leave nor track, nor trace.[5]

This is the more common experience, isn't it? We leave marks on this world, but only the kind that are almost immediately washed away by time. We impact the few people around us;

we make a few lives better; we are faithful with the few talents entrusted to us; and then we are gone. Few of us leave the kind of footprints that will be visible for more than the briefest of moments. Hannah Gould knew this but was unconcerned that she would leave little "track nor trace" of her pilgrimage. She was unconcerned, because she understood that God is creating a different kind of monument, one that is far more lasting.

> And yet, with Him, who counts the sands
> And holds the waters in his hands,
> I know a lasting record stands
> Inscribed against my name,
> Of all, this mortal part has wrought;
> Of all, this thinking soul has thought;
> And from these fleeting moments caught
> For glory or for shame.[6]

What counts in the economy of God is not what other people remember about us or the honors and accolades that follow our passing. There is no connection between the stateliness of the monuments erected for us on earth and the extent of the rewards we receive in heaven. God knows our hearts, he knows our deeds, he knows our loves. He knows what we've done, what we've thought, what we've attempted in the fleeting moments assigned to us, what we still desired to do when we were taken away. That's true if we live years, decades, or centuries.

Nick doesn't need to be remembered by other people, because he will never be forgotten by God. His deeds don't need to be recorded in the annals of history, because his name has been recorded in the Book of Life. He doesn't need a great monument to his name, because he will receive a white stone, with a new name written on the stone that no one knows except he himself and his God.[7] I am certain that neither he nor any of his fellow saints in heaven are proud if their names are still spoken here or even the least bit troubled if they've passed beyond all memory. Rather, he is among that numberless host wishing only that Christ may be known, that Christ may be remembered, that Christ may be honored. And now I pray, may Christ be honored in me until the day comes when I, too, am gone and forgotten here, and when I too have arrived and am remembered there.

well done, good and faithful dad

I know him only by the framed black-and-white photograph that once hung in my grandmother's house and now hangs in my mother's. The picture shows him as a dashing young fighter pilot who had heeded the call to arms and volunteered to serve in the Royal Canadian Air Force. Though his long brown hair is askew, tossed by the wind, it somehow still looks perfect. He casually sits on the cowling of his aircraft, confident, smiling, and prepared. He is ready to do his duty, ready to go to war.

When I was a child, the elderly folk I knew had come of age during the Second World War. Theirs was "The Greatest Generation" and included all those brave boys who had rushed to join up, been shipped off to foreign lands, and had fought terrible battles across land, sea, and air. And though the men I knew eventually returned and built lives for themselves, so many of their peers did not. The man whose portrait hung on the wall did not. In 1944, my great-uncle Harold embarked on a mission and disappeared over the Mediterranean Sea. He was never heard from again.

My childhood hometown, like nearly every other in Canada, had a cenotaph in its town square, a memorial to the men who had fought and died. I would sometimes go there on Remembrance Day, November 11, to participate in ceremonies meant to honor these men and to preserve their memory. My young eyes would look with pity at the tearstained faces of old men and women who stood forlorn, holding faded photographs emblazoned with the traditional poppies—tributes to brothers or fathers who had served and sacrificed, who had died and been laid to rest in the vast burying fields of Western Europe. The men in those photographs were forever frozen in time, as young then as they had been on the day they fell in battle. But each year, the ones holding the photographs grew older, grayer, more stooped, more drawn. I had no category for understanding how, after so many years, their grief could remain so sharp, so raw, so present. I had no category for understanding why, even after so many years, my grandmother could only on the rarest of occasions bring herself to speak of her brother.

But I am beginning to understand. I am beginning to understand that some wounds never truly heal, that some burdens weigh heavy for a lifetime, that some of God's providences cut so deep that to even think of them is to stir up all the old emotion, and to speak of them is to provoke all the old pain. Some sorrows will only be comforted in the place where all tears are dried.

When the Lord granted me a son as my firstborn child,

I formed a vision in my mind of growing old with him at my side. In that vision, I was bent and gray-haired, very near to the end of my time on earth. I was lying on a bed with my family gathered by my side. Nick took my hand, and as I slipped from earth to heaven, I heard him whisper, "Well done, good and faithful dad!"—a human affirmation of the divine blessing I long to hear from Jesus when I arrive in heaven. That vision gave birth to purpose. "The glory of children is their fathers,"[1] says Solomon, and I determined I would live before my son as a worthy example of a man, a husband, a father, and a Christian. I would live a life of such wisdom and godliness that Nick would be proud to be related to me, proud to call me his dad, proud to be with me at the end. While I knew that ultimately I must live for the glory of God and for his commendation, I was determined to live in such an upright and honorable way that I would also receive Nick's.

But then that vision was over. I'm still determined to live a life worthy of the gospel of Jesus Christ. It's just that Nick will no longer be there beside me, here to witness my death and take my hand and whisper those words at the end. He no longer needs me to lead the way, to show him how to succeed in life, in ministry, in marriage, and in family. And so instead of my life being an example to him, it has become a tribute. I don't know if he can see what is happening here on earth, or if he perhaps receives reports or dispatches that keep him informed. The Bible is not clear on that. But I have chosen to live as if he does, as if he is cheering me on, as if I can continue to make him proud that he is my son, that I am his father.

Last night, as I lay in that state that exists somewhere between awake and asleep, I caught a new vision of myself—a vision of myself as one of those sorrowful old men holding a faded, framed photograph of a much younger man. Time has moved on, but he has not, for in the picture he is still just twenty years old, the same age he was when I last saw him, last hugged him, last told him I loved him. I have celebrated many birthdays since then; he has celebrated none. My face is weathered and creased; his remains young and fresh. Few now remember his name, and fewer still the sound of his voice, the cackle of his laugh, the sparkle of his eyes. But as I gaze fondly at his familiar form, I remember it all. Though the years have given way to decades, though so much has changed within and without, he is still alive in my mind and still present in my heart. My love burns as strong as ever.

I once read an author's description of a time he and his family embarked on a fishing excursion. They set out in the morning, and as they made their way toward open waters, they came upon a series of small islands. His son asked if he could explore one of them until the family returned that way later in the day, then clambered out of the boat while the rest of the party continued on toward the nearby fishing grounds. As afternoon turned to evening and they began the return journey, darkness fell and a thick fog settled in. The father became uncertain of the direction, so he slowly groped his way along the coast until he could hear the sound of the surf breaking on the islands. However, with all the mist he was at a loss to know which was the island on which his child awaited. And so he went to the bow, cupped his hands around his mouth, and began to shout into the darkness. Far off in the distance he heard his son's faint reply carrying over the waters: "Father, I am here! Come toward me! I'm waiting for you!" He steered in the direction of that voice, calling and then listening, until the boat finally touched the shore and his son leaped into his arms, exclaiming, "I knew you would find me, father!"[2]

In my own vision, I am aboard a similar vessel far out to sea, that precious photograph still clasped tightly in my arms. The weather-beaten little boat has endured many storms, many great tempests that have nearly flooded it, many great waves that have nearly washed over it. And now, with land fading into the distance behind me, I begin to hear a far-off cry: "I'm here dad! Steer toward my voice. I'm waiting for you!" The voice comes from the direction of faith, the direction of sanctification, the direction of perseverance. It comes from the direction of heaven. And so, through the mists, I make my way toward it, holding my course toward the sound of Nick's voice. "Steady on now," I hear him call. "Don't give up! You're getting closer." His voice grows louder in my ear as I close the distance between us.

And then as my boat finally nudges up against the shores of a land so fair, I find him waiting for me there—there in that place where the last enemy has been defeated, where Death itself has been put to death, where nothing ever can, or ever will, separate us again. "I knew you would find me!" he says. Then as he throws his arms around me, he speaks the words I have waited so long to hear: "Well done, good and faithful dad!"

the final first

The air is again blowing colder, the nights again growing longer. The leaves of the great oak and maple that tower over our home have already turned vibrant shades of red, yellow, and orange, then drifted to the ground below. We are not far from the first frost, not far from the first snow, not far from one year fading into the next.

In the earliest days of our grief, when our minds were so bewildered and our hearts so shattered, we were told that this year would be the most difficult of all because it would be the year of so many firsts—the first day and night of mourning, the first holiday feast with a chair left conspicuously empty, the first Christmas with two stockings by the fire instead of three, the first birthday when Nick would not age by one year or even one day. Each of these firsts would bring its own grief, we were told—each its fresh sorrow. The words proved true, for as often as not, occasions on the calendar that would otherwise have brought special joy have brought sharp pain.

Today we have come to another first—to the final first—for today is the anniversary of Nick's death. I've heard some refer to this as a "deathday," a term that morbidly parallels "birthday." But I prefer to stick with the wordier, more formal "anniversary of his death." It was one year ago today that we received the news he had collapsed, one year ago today that our lives were turned upside down, one year ago today that in the dark skies over Ohio I inadvertently began writing through the seasons of my sorrow.

We gathered at the cemetery this evening to mark the occasion. With a few friends and a few family members, we stood by Nick's grave and sang together—songs that gave words to our sorrow, our praise, our expectation. We sang of the grace that has brought us safe thus far and the grace that will lead us home.[1] We declared that whatever our lot, God has taught us to say, "It is well, it is well with my soul."[2] With tears in our eyes, we proclaimed our sure and steady hope that on a day known to only God himself, we will feast together in the house of Zion and recount the great and mighty deeds of our God—that day when we will weep no more.[3]

With the daylight fading fast around us, we sang, we prayed, we hugged, and we returned to the warmth of our home.

A friend recently asked what I have learned through this hardest of all years. I had no great answer for him at the time, but this evening it seems all too clear: "to work and to weep." This, it seems, is what constitutes life on this side of glory. We journey to heaven working and weeping. Yes, there are times of rest and times of joy as well—"A time to weep, and a time to laugh; a time to mourn, and a time to dance."[4] But every joy is tempered by sorrow, every moment of rest by the knowledge that the work must still go on. The purest joy and fullest rest always lie beyond time's horizon.

Jesus once encountered a group of men who insisted they

wished to follow him and be his disciples. But Jesus knew the hearts of men, so he warned them to first carefully count the cost.[5] It became clear soon enough that they would follow him only if they could retain their comfortable lives, only if they could follow at their own convenience, only if they could follow as a matter of secondary priority. Turning to his disciples, Jesus said, "No one who puts his hand to the plow and looks back is fit for the kingdom of God."[6] This was a call to dedication and perseverance, for the farmer who plows with his eyes behind him will inevitably cut furrows that are jagged, sloppy, shameful. The only way for him to cut a straight furrow is to set his eye on a distant point and to keep it fixed there until he has finally arrived at the edge of his field.

At those few farms that still surround this town, the farmers recently harvested their summer crop. But even with the harvest gathered in, and even with their barns full, it was not yet time to rest, for they still had to put their hand to the plow and labor until they had prepared for the next season. And so their tractors once again crisscrossed their fields; they once again sowed their seed; they once again planted their crop—the wheat that will lie dormant through the long winter before it finally bursts to life with the first rays of the warm spring sun.

Like those farmers, I know that arriving at the end of one season has merely brought me to the dawn of another. It is not yet time to rest, for there is still work I need to do, still seeds to sow and a harvest to reap—a harvest of Christian graces, of faithful living, of love and good deeds. So I must put my hand to the plow and keep looking forward rather than back.

If the way forward leads the farmer to the end of his field and a winter's rest, my way forward leads me to the end of my life and to eternal rest. It leads me to the day when death shall be no more, when mourning, crying, pain, and all such things will have passed away.[7] That day is coming, but it is not here yet. Even as I put my hand to the plow, it can only ever be one hand, for I will need the other to dry my eyes. To keep one hand on the plow while wiping away tears with the other—this is the essence of living and laboring as a Christian.[8] So I will press on and not look back. I've set my glistening eyes to heaven, my eyes to the end of my journey, my eyes to my great reward, and I will move steadily toward it. By God's grace, I'll work and I'll weep until I finally arrive in the place of comfort, the place of rest, the place that is most truly my home.

———

The sun has set, the house has fallen quiet, and it is time for me to retire for the night. I'll go upstairs now and slip into the room where Aileen is already at rest. I'll roll over to be close to her and lie there for a few minutes, listening to the sound of her breathing, until my chest begins to rise and fall in unison with hers. My eyes will grow heavy and my mind will grow hazy. Soon enough I, too, will drift off. And as one day fades into the next, I'll sleep, confident in the knowledge that when I awake with the sun, I will be one day nearer to heaven, one day nearer to Jesus, and one day nearer to Nick. "Good night, my boy," I'll whisper into the darkness. "Good night, till then."

IN MEMORY OF

Nick Challies (2000–2020)

author note

In the immediate aftermath of Nick's death I found myself craving the company of those who had walked this path before me. I turned to authors from bygone eras, for while the loss of a child is strange to us, it was familiar to so many of them. Many of the reflections in this book were inspired by words, phrases, sentences, or ideas from authors like J. R. Miller, F. B. Meyer, Theodore Cuyler, Thomas Smyth, P. B. Power, Thomas De Witt Talmage, John Flavel, and others. They, almost as much as any living men or women, have been my companions through this year. I have done my best to note anything I drew from them but have undoubtedly missed some. After reading so many thousands of pages of their words, I sometimes struggle to separate their thoughts from mine. I trust they, and you, will forgive me for any I've failed to cite.

acknowledgments

Aileen, Abby, Michaela, and Ryn—I am so proud of you and so thankful for you. Let's do what we've promised even when Nick was still with us—let's stay true to the Lord and true to his Word, so we can all look forward to a great reunion in heaven. What a day that will be!

I need to express gratitude to my mother, sisters, and brother, as well as Aileen's parents and sister for all the ways they supported us through our loss and through the year that followed. And I need to express gratitude to the many people in our neighborhood who were so kind, helpful, and generous. We couldn't have done it without you.

In the very early days, we received extraordinary and unforgettable help from so many of the staff, faculty, and students at Boyce College and the Southern Baptist Theological Seminary, and also from the pastors and members of Third Avenue Baptist Church. I am so grateful. I am grateful as well for the dear brothers and sisters at Grace Fellowship Church who took such good care of us. Special thanks also to Scott and Mona,

John and Milly, Curtis and Jenny, Paul and Susan, Aaron, and Chris, each of whom served us in exceptional ways. And then I must offer thanks to the many readers of my blog who reached out with condolences and prayers.

The Lord arranged for us to get to know other parents who are part of the sacred circle of the sorrowing, and I'm thankful for friendships with Robb and Karen, Jamie and Vanessa, James and Mary, and Joel and Danielle. Your faith and endurance have blessed us in so many ways.

I'm grateful to the teams at Wolgemuth & Associates and Zondervan Reflective for their support of this project.

If you have been in any way moved, helped, or blessed by this book, please consider making a donation to the scholarship that is distributed to students at Boyce College and Southern Seminary who plan to take up the ministry Nick was not able to—ministering the gospel of Jesus Christ within Canada. You can learn more about it at www.sbts.edu/support /challiesscholarship.

notes

Chapter 3: In the Deepest Darkness

1. See Jeff Robinson, "Heartbroken Boyce College Students Mourn the Abrupt Death of Nick Challies," *Southern News*, November 4, 2020, news .sbts.edu/2020/11/04/heartbroken-boyce-college-students-mourn-the -abrupt-death-of-nick-challies.

2. See Theodore L. Cuyler, *God's Light on Dark Clouds* (London: Hodder & Stoughton, 1882), 45. The rowing metaphor I use here is also inspired by Cuyler and an essay ("Christ's Hand at the Helm") in Theodore Cuyler, *Mountain Tops with Jesus: Calls to a Higher Life* (New York: Revell, 1899), 28–34.

3. This final line is inspired by J. R. Miller, *Week-Day Religion* (London: Hodder & Stoughton, 1898), 273.

Chapter 4: Good Night, Till Then

1. Leonhard Sturm, "Good Night, Till Then," trans. Jane Borthwick, Hymnary .org, accessed April 19, 2022, https://hymnary.org/text/i_journey_forth _rejoicing. Public domain.

Chapter 5: From Grave to Glory

1. John 12:24.

2. 1 Corinthians 15:36.

3. See 1 Corinthians 15:42–43.

4. Paraphrased from the Apostles' Creed.

5. See Genesis 8:22.

6. We will allow the exceptions of Enoch and Elijah to prove the rule.

Chapter 6: Asleep in Jesus

1. John 11:11; Acts 7:60; 1 Corinthians 15:18.
2. Ben Jonson, "On My First Son," Poetry Foundation, accessed April 19, 2022, www.poetryfoundation.org/poems/44455/on-my-first-son.
3. Luke 23:43.
4. Philippians 1:21.
5. See 1 Thessalonians 4:16.
6. See 1 Corinthians 16:22; Revelation 22:20.

Chapter 7: God Is Good All the Time

1. The first anecdote I heard long ago but cannot now place; the second is widely attributed to Karl Barth.
2. This is widely attributed to Charles Spurgeon, but I've had trouble tracing it to its original source.
3. See "Lord's Day 10" (Q&A 27), Heidelberg-Catechism.com, Canadian Reformed Theological Seminary, accessed April 19, 2022, www.heidel berg-catechism.com/en/lords-days/10.html.
4. Job 1:21.
5. See Wayne Grudem, *Systematic Theology: An Introduction to Biblical Doctrine*, 2nd ed. (1994; repr., Grand Rapids: Zondervan, 2020), 236–37.

Chapter 8: Only Ever an Onlooker

1. See Hebrews 12:6.
2. See Galatians 5:22–23.
3. Kathrina von Schlegel, "Be Still, My Soul," trans. Jane Borthwick, Hymnary.org, accessed April 19, 2022, https://hymnary.org/text/be_still _my_soul_the_lord_is_on_thy_side. Public domain.

Chapter 9: My Manifesto

1. See 1 Corinthians 15:58.
2. See Philippians 3:14.
3. See Hebrews 12:1–2.
4. See 2 Timothy 4:7.

Chapter 10: Singing in the Dark

1. Proverbs 14:10.
2. See Jeremiah 17:10; Isaiah 53:3; Romans 8:26.
3. Charles Spurgeon, "Man Unknown to Man," Metropolitan Tabernacle

Pulpit vol. 35, April 14, 1889, The Spurgeon Center, accessed April 19, 2022, www.spurgeon.org/resource-library/sermons/man-unknown-to-man.

4. My gratitude goes to Chris Mouring, who in private correspondence drew the distinction between "getting on with it" and "getting over it."

Chapter 11: I Fear God and I'm Afraid of God

1. See Proverbs 9:10.
2. See R. C. Sproul, *Now, That's a Good Question!* (Wheaton, IL: Tyndale, 1996), 17–18.
3. Psalm 112:1.

Chapter 12: Turning to Face the Sun

1. This illustration was inspired by Theodore L. Cuyler, *Wayside Springs from the Fountain of Life* (London: Hodder & Stoughton, 1883), 101–6.
2. See Psalm 34:15, 18.
3. See James 1:17, Malachi 3:6, Hebrews 13:8.
4. See Genesis 8:22.
5. See John 14:26.
6. Psalm 37:25.
7. See Psalm 84:11.
8. See Malachi 4:2.

Chapter 13: Help My Unbelief!

1. See Mark 9:14–29.
2. "1689 Baptist Confession Chapter 31," ARBCA, accessed April 19, 2022, www.arbca.com/1689-chapter31.

Chapter 14: What Do You Do with Grief?

1. Colossians 3:5.
2. Colossians 3:12.
3. See Philippians 3:13–14.

Chapter 15: Crying Eyes and Smiling Hearts

1. See Ephesians 6:4.

Chapter 17: Stewarding Sorrow

1. See Matthew 25:14–30.

2. Maltbie D. Babcock, "This Is My Father's World," Hymnary.org, accessed April 19, 2022, https://hymnary.org/text/this_is_my_fathers_world _and_to_my. Public domain.

Chapter 18: Thy Will Be Done

1. Luke 22:42.
2. The phrases "shed tears over sorrows that may never come" and "slow suicide" were used by the nineteenth-century Presbyterian minister and religious writer Theodore Cuyler in a number of his works.
3. Matthew 6:34.
4. See Horatio Spafford, "When Peace, Like a River," Hymnary.org, accessed April 19, 2022, https://hymnary.org/text/when_peace_like_a_river _attendeth_my_way. Public domain.

Chapter 19: To My Son on His Twenty-First Birthday

1. Theodore Cuyler wrote various versions of this phrase in his books and sermons.
2. 1 Corinthians 15:22.
3. See James 4:14.

Chapter 20: Homesick

1. See Revelation 21:15–23.
2. See John 14:2; 2 Corinthians 5:8.
3. Inspired by T. De Witt Talmage, *Trumpet Peals: A Collection of Timely and Eloquent Extracts* (New York: Bromfield, 1890), 462.

Chapter 21: Flowers in the Desert

1. See Romans 8:28.
2. John 13:7.
3. See Genesis 45:5; 50:20; Acts 4:28.
4. I first encountered the idea of "afterward promises" in the writings of the Presbyterian pastor, author, and editor J. R. Miller; see his chapter 8 in *Silent Times: A Book to Help in Reading the Bible into Life* (New York: Ward & Drummond, 1886), 84–92, https://springsofgrace.church/2021/03/afterward.
5. See Acts 7:54–60; 12:6–19; Revelation 1:9–11.
6. See William Cowper, "God Moves in a Mysterious Way," Hymnal.net, accessed April 19, 2022, www.hymnal.net/en/hymn/h/675. Public domain.
7. See Romans 8:28 NIV.

Chapter 22: Not a Moment Too Early

1. Matthew 13:3, 24; John 4:35.
2. See Genesis 5:24.

Chapter 23: How Long Is the Dash?

1. John 16:16.

Chapter 24: An Empty Room

1. See Thomas Smyth, *The Complete Works of Thomas Smyth*, vol. 10 (Columbia, SC: R. L. Bryan, 1912), 20–21, http://library.logcollegepress .com/Smyth%2C+Volume+10.pdf.

Chapter 25: How Many Children Do I Have?

1. Adapted and paraphrased from Mark 12:18–27.
2. See Tim Challies and Jules Koblun, *Knowing and Enjoying God* (Eugene, OR: Harvest House, 2021).

Chapter 26: The Cause of Death

1. See 1 Samuel 2:6.
2. Psalm 115:3.
3. Job 12:10, emphasis added.

Chapter 27: The Trumpet Shall Sound

1. All quotes from Handel's *Messiah* in this chapter are taken from Charles Morris, "Handel's Messiah: Lyrics and Verse References," Haven Today, November 20, 2020, https://haventoday.org/blog/handels-messiah-lyrics -verse-references.
2. 1 Thessalonians 4:16.
3. 1 Corinthians 15:52.
4. Luke 17:24.

Chapter 28: Follow in My Footsteps

1. See Adelaide Rodham, *The Footsteps of Christ* (Edinburgh: T&T Clark, 1871), 318.
2. Carrie Ellis Breck, "Face to Face with Christ My Savior," Hymnary.org, accessed April 19, 2022, https://hymnary.org/text/face_to_face_with _christ_my_savior. Public domain.
3. See 2 Corinthians 5:8.

Chapter 29: The Sacred Circle

1. Charles Spurgeon, "Man Unknown to Man," Metropolitan Tabernacle Pulpit vol. 35, April 14, 1889, The Spurgeon Center, accessed April 19, 2022, www.spurgeon.org/resource-library/sermons/man-unknown-to-man, emphasis added.

2. 2 Samuel 12:7 KJV.

3. Charles Wesley, "Death of a Child," Hymnary.org, accessed April 19, 2022, https://hymnary.org/text/wherefore_should_i_make_my_moan. Public domain.

4. Henry Wadsworth Longfellow, "Resignation," Henry Wadsworth Longfellow (website), Maine Historical Society, accessed April 19, 2022, www.hwlongfellow.org/poems_poem.php?pid=117. Public domain.

5. Miss H. F. Gould, "The Child of a Year and a Day," in *Poems*, vol. 3 (Boston: Hilliard, Gray, 1853), 35.

6. Fanny Crosby, *Fanny Crosby's Story of Ninety-Four Years*, retold by S. Trevena Jackson (New York: Revell, 1915), 57.

7. You can read brief accounts of many of these people in James W. Bruce III, *From Grief to Glory* (Edinburgh: Banner of Truth, 2008)—a book that would have saved me a lot of time had I read it before doing all the research for this chapter.

8. Among the historic books specific to grieving a child are Thomas Smyth, *Solace for Bereaved Parents* (New York: Carter, 1848); William Logan, *Words of Comfort for Parents Bereaved of Little Children* (London: Nisbet, 1867); Theodore L. Cuyler, *The Empty Crib: A Memorial of Little Georgie, with Words of Consolation for Bereaved Parents* (New York: Carter and Brothers, 1868); and N. W. Wilder, ed., *Little Graves: Choice Selections of Poetry and Prose* (New York: Nelson & Phillips, 1876). More recent books include Nicholas Wolterstorff, *Lament for a Son* (Grand Rapids: Eerdmans, 1987); Jerry Sittser, *A Grace Disguised: How the Soul Grows through Loss* (1995; repr., Grand Rapids: Zondervan, 2021); and Nancy Guthrie, *Holding On to Hope: A Pathway through Suffering to the Heart of God* (Wheaton, IL: Tyndale, 2002).

9. Attributed to one of Theodore Cuyler's acquaintances in Cuyler, *The Empty Crib*, 102.

10. See Hebrews 10:24 NIV; Revelation 21:4.

Chapter 30: Angels Unaware

1. Psalm 37:25.

2. Proverbs 10:1 NIV.
3. See Luke 2:52.
4. Proverbs 29:3.
5. 1 Thessalonians 5:23–24, 28.

Chapter 31: On the Other Side of the Wall

1. Inspired by Alice Cary's poem "April," in which these lines appear: "So, even for the dead I will not bind my soul to grief: Death cannot long divide; for is it not as if the rose that climbed my garden wall, had bloomed the other side?" Found in Katharine Lee Bates, ed., *The Poems of Alice and Phoebe Cary* (New York: Crowell, 1903), 261.
2. See Luke 2:52.
3. The final sentence is drawn from P. B. Power, *A Book of Comfort for Those in Sickness* (1876; repr., Edinburgh: Banner of Truth, 2018), 97.

Chapter 32: Courage, Dear Heart

1. C. S. Lewis, *The Voyage of the Dawn Treader* (1952; repr., New York: HarperCollins, 1994), 186–87.

Chapter 33: The Ministry of Sorrow

1. J. R. Miller, *The Ministry of Comfort* (London: Hodder & Stoughton, 1903), 14.
2. Adapted from J. R. Miller, "As Living Stones" (entry in section 2), in *The Garden of the Heart*, Grace Gems, accessed April 19, 2022, https://gracegems.org/Miller/garden_of_the_heart.htm.
3. See Ephesians 2:20.
4. Judson W. Van De Venter, "I Surrender All," Hymnary.org, accessed April 19, 2022, https://hymnary.org/text/all_to_jesus_i_surrender. Public domain
5. Frances R. Havergal, "Take My Life and Let It Be," Hymnary.org, accessed April 19, 2022, https://hymnary.org/text/take_my_life_and_let_it_be. Public domain.
6. See 2 Corinthians 1:4.
7. See Galatians 6:2.
8. See Romans 12:15.

Chapter 34: God, Give Me Sons

1. Proverbs 15:20 NIV.

2. And indeed Abby was married to Nathan Elfarrah on May 15, 2022, just after I completed this manuscript.

Chapter 35: In Green Pastures

1. Psalm 23:1.
2. Psalm 23:4.
3. Isaiah 46:10.
4. Psalm 23:6.
5. The inspiration for these thoughts come, in part, from J. R. Miller, *By the Still Waters: A Meditation on the Twenty-Third Psalm* (New York: Crowell, 1898), www.gracegems.org/Miller/still_waters.htm.

Chapter 36: My Most Precious Possession

1. Story summarized from Theodore L. Cuyler, *The Empty Crib* (New York: R. Carter and Brothers, 1868), 76.
2. You can learn about many of these Bibles in my book and video series titled *Epic: An Around-the-World Journey through Christian History* (Grand Rapids: Zondervan Reflective, 2020).
3. 1 Corinthians 15:22.

Chapter 37: Nothing He Needs

1. 2 Samuel 9:8 NIV.
2. 2 Samuel 9:1.
3. See James 1:27.
4. See Revelation 6:10.

Chapter 39: Death Did Him No Harm

1. John Donne, "Holy Sonnets: Death, Be Not Proud," Poetry Foundation, accessed April 19, 2022, www.poetryfoundation.org/poems/44107/holy -sonnets-death-be-not-proud. Public domain.
2. See 1 Corinthians 15:26.
3. This chapter was inspired in part by pastor Tim Binion who, at the funeral of Grace Keen (July 10, 2001–March 18, 2021), testified that "death did her no harm."

Chapter 40: It's Time to Rise!

1. C. S. Lewis, *The Voyage of the Dawn Treader* (1952; repr., New York: HarperCollins, 1994), 187.
2. 1 Thessalonians 4:16–17.

Chapter 41: Footprints on the Sands of Time

1. Henry Wadsworth Longfellow, "A Psalm of Life," Poetry Foundation, accessed April 19, 2022, www.poetryfoundation.org/poems/44644 /a-psalm-of-life. Public domain.
2. J. Hart, "Come, Ye Sinners, Poor and Needy," Hymnary.org, accessed April 19, 2022, https://hymnary.org/text/come_ye_sinners_poor_and _needy_weak_and. Public domain.
3. Isaac Watts, "Joy to the World, the Lord Is Come!" Hymnary.org, accessed April 19, 2022, https://hymnary.org/text/joy_to_the_world_the_lord _is_come. Public domain.
4. Longfellow, "A Psalm of Life."
5. Miss H. F. Gould, "A Name in the Sand," in *Poems*, vol. 3 (Boston: Hilliard, Gray, 1853), 34.
6. Gould, "A Name in the Sand."
7. See Revelation 2:17.

Chapter 42: Well Done, Good and Faithful Dad

1. Proverbs 17:6.
2. See Thomas Smyth, *The Complete Works of Thomas Smyth*, vol. 10 (Columbia, SC: R.L. Bryan, 1912), 210.

Epilogue

1. See John Newton, "Amazing Grace! (How Sweet the Sound)," Hymnary .org, accessed April 19, 2022, https://hymnary.org/text/amazing_grace _how_sweet_the_sound. Public domain.
2. Horatio Spafford, "When Peace, Like a River," Hymnary.org, accessed April 19, 2022, https://hymnary.org/text/when_peace_like_a_river _attendeth_my_way. Public domain.
3. See Sandra McCracken and Joshua Moore, "We Will Feast in the House of Zion," track 2 on *Psalms*, 2015, https://sandramccracken.bandcamp .com/track/we-will-feast-in-the-house-of-zion.
4. Ecclesiastes 3:4.
5. See Luke 9:57–62; 14:25–33.
6. Luke 9:62.
7. See Revelation 21:4.
8. I have variously heard this phrase attributed to the Puritans and to Watchman Nee. Thanks to Maryanne for bringing it to my attention.